P9-APH-347

PRAISE FOR
MARKETING FOR PEOPLE *NOT* IN MARKETING

"The concept that marketing is everybody's job—that the market is the source of jobs and should therefore be our focal point—is the ultimate driver of profits. Attention to this credo and to this book should be paid."
— Mack Hanan, *Consultative Selling*

"What an ideal book—easy to read, fun, and LOTS of practical, useful information. This book has what I call 'put into practice today' ideas."
— Donna Fisher, *Power Networking: 55 Secrets for Personal & Professional Success*

"This book will open the door to the fun and profits of marketing your business."
— Lawrence M. Kohn, *Selling With Honor: Strategies for Selling Without Selling Your Soul*

"The vast majority of future sales will come from current customers. Building relationships is clearly the direction that all companies should be going."
— Paul Timm, *50 Powerful Ideas You Can Use to Keep Your Customers*

"Rick Crandall's done it again! A terrific primer for people whose only marketing experience is at the 7-11. Packed with accessible and practical information."
— David Brandt, PhD, *Sacred Cows Make the Best Burgers*

"Since all the world is a marketing problem, this book should be an invaluable aid."
— Jack Trout, *The New Positioning*

"Great information! Everyone should read this book—and profit from it."
— Bob Burg, *Endless Referrals: Network Your Everyday Contacts into Sales* and *Winning WITHOUT Intimidation*

"This superb book drove me up one quantum leap in my personal performance. It applies the Golden Rule to selling and marketing. I've already put four new ideas to work. Highly readable."
— Alan W. Cundall, creative director emeritus, Hayes Orlie Cundall Inc. Advertising Agency

"A treasure trove of effective ways all employees can use to gain and hold customers."
— Mel Mandell, *The Cost Curmudgeon,* and *1001 Ways to Operate Your Business More Profitably*

"Successful marketing is more about *farming* than it is about *hunting. Marketing for People not in Marketing* shows how anyone can cultivate relationships and harvest more business."
— Ivan R. Misner, PhD, founder of BNI, *The World's Best Known Marketing Secret*

"Finally—a to-the-point, concise, and impactful sales and marketing book that's easy to understand and apply, and written by experts who know what serves the customer. I especially liked Bill Blade's section on servant selling."
— Conrad J. Hunter, area general manager, Cellular One/GTE Mid South Business Sales & Major Accounts

"This latest in a series of valuable marketing tools from the Institute for Effective Marketing is readable, entertaining, and filled with sound recommendations for developing long-term relationships with customers. Anyone interested in starting or building a business should read this book."
— Ronald E. Goldsmith, professor, Marketing Department, Florida State University

MARKETING
FOR PEOPLE *NOT* IN
MARKETING

How Everyone Can Build Customer Relationships

Featuring chapters from experts—

Richard A. Blabolil • Bill Blades
Rick Crandall • Elaine C. Dumler • Linda F. Fracassi
Christian Frederiksen • Theodore W. Garrison III
Ed Peters • Jim Rhode

EDITED BY RICK CRANDALL
Illustrations by Monika Chovanec

Sponsored by the
Institute for Effective Marketing

The goal of the Institute for Effective Marketing is to provide information to help organizations and individuals more effectively market their products and services by better serving the needs of their customers.

Select Press
P.O. Box 37
Corte Madera, CA 94976-0037
(415) 924-1612

Marketing for People Not in Marketing: How Everyone Can Build Customer Relationships / Rick Crandall (editor)
Illustrations by Monika Chovanec

ISBN 0-9644294-8-9

Printed in the United States of America
10 9 8 7 6 5 4 3 2 1

Contents

Marketing Systems to Reward Employees and Build Your Business

Preface

Sixty percent or more of your future business should come from current customers. In many successful companies, it's over 90 percent! In the world of the future, people expect one-to-one, personalized products and services at mass market prices. The only way to achieve value in this new competitive marketplace is for everyone in the organization to build relationships with customers—which is the best marketing.

When Nordstrom calls you because new items of a type you like are in, that's customer service—but it also increases sales. When you act as a free consultant to solve customers' problems, and then they pay you for more help, that's relationship building, service, and selling.

Your job is to help people trust you by being trustworthy and communicating clearly. That's relationship building. That's sales and marketing!

— Rick Crandall, PhD
Editor

Chapter 1

WHY MARKETING IS FOR EVERYONE

Rick Crandall

Rick Crandall, PhD, is a speaker, writer, and consultant, specializing in talks and workshops on marketing, sales, and change. He has spoken for *Inc.* magazine, the American Marketing Association, Autodesk, Office Depot, and the American Society for Training and Development. Dr. Crandall has presented well over 1,000 public seminars, given many keynote presentations, and worked with organizations from large law firms to the Air Force.

He is the author of *Marketing Your Services: For People Who HATE to Sell* (1996), *1001 Ways to Market Your Services* (1998) and editor of *Thriving on Change in Organizations* (1997). In addition, he serves as editor and marketing columnist for *Executive Edge* (a national management newsletter).

Dr. Crandall is the recipient of an SBA Small Business Award, and is listed in various *Who's Whos*.

Rick Crandall, PhD; Agent: Select Press, PO Box 37, Corte Madera, CA 94976-0037; phone (415) 924-1612; fax (415) 924-7179; e-mail SelectPr@aol.com.

WHY MARKETING IS FOR EVERYONE

Rick Crandall

> "The purpose of a business is to create a customer...it's not enough to have a strong sales force and entrust marketing to it. Marketing is not a specialized activity...it is the whole business seen from...the customer's point of view."
>
> —Peter Drucker

The most important thing you do in your work is marketing, whether you're in a profit or non-profit organization!

You may *think* you disagree with this statement, but perhaps that's because you have a misconception of what marketing is.

- Marketing is helping, not hard selling.
- Marketing is listening, not lying.
- Marketing is serving others, not conning them.
- Marketing is friendly advice, not fast talking.
- Marketing is finding people who need what you offer, not fooling them into buying what you want to sell.

In this book, we share a general definition of marketing (with occasional side excursions). Marketing is anything you do to get *or* keep a customer. It includes advertising, sales, and publicity—functions that are used to get customers, and are traditionally thought of as marketing. But the most important part of marketing is customer service. That's what you do to *keep* customers.

EVERYBODY MARKETS

No organization succeeds unless it serves its customers well. If you have contact with customers, or support those who do (your internal customers), you can make a difference to customer service and the income and success of your organization.

In most businesses, repeat business should be high because repeat business is very profitable. An FMI Consulting study showed that *average* construction companies had 60 percent repeat business over time, but that *successful* companies had 90 percent repeat business! Another study showed that for every 5 percent increase in client retention, profits went up between 25 and 100 percent.

GREAT CUSTOMER SERVICE

↓

SATISFIED CUSTOMERS

REFERRALS   REPEAT BUSINESS

INCREASED BUSINESS

Besides the value of repeat business gained through great customer service, satisfied clients also bring referral business. Referrals are the most effective way to find new clients—and the least expensive.

SERVING CUSTOMERS BETTER

From the customers' point of view, there's a big difference between the bank teller who is "professionally friendly" and someone who remembers customers' names and enjoys talking with them.

Looking at internal customers, take the example of a company bookkeeper who provides line-of-business breakdowns for the sales department. Some bookkeepers grudgingly and bureaucratically do the minimum necessary—when they get around to it. Others cooperate in any way they can. It's obvious who helps their companies the most, builds morale, and contributes to the success of the overall organization.

Nonmarketers Are Better Marketers

Often people whose job titles don't involve sales or marketing are more potent marketers than those with the marketing job titles. Many medical office patients interact more with the receptionist than they do with the doctor. Remembering customers' names, offering smiles and conversation, and cheerfully working with a patient to find a convenient time for a return visit can make a big impression.

Or take the computer tech support person or phone installer. When they give the customer advice, it has more credibility than the same information coming from the marketing department, because they're not "selling."

On the other hand, when they make an offhand comment about how fouled up the company support is, they're killing future sales.

Here's an example of great marketing that most traditional business gurus wouldn't even

---

Reception = Customer Service

Most companies hire receptionists and similar positions as administrative staff. Yet these positions have big impacts on customers. Why not follow the lead of companies who staff reception by using rotating customer service staff at the front desk? This makes it clear that greeting customers is a customer service function.

—Jack Burke,
Creating Customer Connections

count as marketing. A friend of mine had an old pair of binoculars that he had taken to San Francisco 49er football games for 20 years. Eventually one side of the strap broke. He went to a store where he regularly shopped that carried cases with the goal of buying a new snap-on strap. Store personnel recommended that instead of buying a new strap, he have the old one sewed to the case by the neighborhood shoe repair store. He did, and saved $25.

I'd say that his regular store gave up a short-term sale, and built their long-term relationship while generating word-of-mouth referrals. That's real marketing.

NONPROFITS MARKET TOO

Most people associate marketing with commercial enterprises. However, most of the points in this book apply equally well to selling your ideas to others, running a charity, or convincing your kids to do their homework. The principles of helping others, building relationships, and using your expertise apply.

Let's say you're a nonprofit organization. Your customers include the people you serve, your donors, your volunteers, and probably a government agency or two.

I once volunteered my time to call a charity's past donors to ask them to pledge again. If the donor said no, I didn't feel bad—I figured the decision had nothing to do with me. And when I explained that I was a volunteer, and had made a donation during the last fundraiser just as they did, many thanked me for taking the time to call.

If you're not a nonprofit, your customers can still be pleased that you called them if you have their good at heart. That's why Nordstrom's customers like being told when new items in their favorite lines come in.

"Marketing is also in not-for-profit organizations.... [For instance] in a United Way campaign, contributors of money gain good feelings and reduce their guilt in return for their money."
Thomas C. Kinnear and Kenneth L. Bernhardt, *Principles of Marketing*

WHAT'S IN IT FOR YOU?

Maybe you'll agree that marketing, defined mainly as taking good care of customers, sounds okay. But what's really in it for you?

In the chart to the left, you can see that the benefits you receive from marketing are surprisingly similar, whether you own a business or are an employee.

The comparisons when dealing with internal customers are similar. The colleague who is a "good marketer" is fun to work with and builds morale. The internal "bad marketer" is a jerk who takes the fun out of work with bureaucracy, internal politics, and backbiting!

Benefits of Marketing

FOR OWNERS	FOR EMPLOYEES
• make profits	• possible profit sharing
• make income secure	• make job secure
• support other interests	• support other interests
• choose who you work with	• choose where you work
• meet more people	• meet more people
• get out of office	• get out of office
• deductible lunches/ entertainment	• deductible lunches/ entertainment
• learn about different businesses	• learn about different businesses
• achieve goals/ meet challenges	• achieve goals/ meet challenges
• create a business	• create a career
• support employees	• support work team
• learn new skills	• learn new skills

WHY PEOPLE DISLIKE MARKETING

If the list of benefits for marketing is so long, why don't more people do it?

A big reason most people don't like the idea of marketing is because they think of it as selling. Sales (and to some degree marketing) has a bad image in our culture. When I looked up the word "sell" in my children's dictionary, the sample sentences were "Sell out your cause" and "Sell your soul to the devil." Even worse, when I looked up the word "pushy," the sample sentence was "A pushy salesman!"

As you'll see in other chapters, being pushy is not what sales is about. It's about serving others, building relationships, and using your expertise to help people meet their needs.

What's Holding You Back?

Perhaps some of these reasons are hurting your motivation to market:

(1) it distracts from my "real" work
(2) fear of rejection by strangers
(3) fear of imposing on others
(4) sleazy image of selling
(5) pressure to produce results

Dislike of marketing is largely emotional, so giving reasons why you shouldn't feel that way will not immediately increase your liking of it. However, lets look at some ways you can change your feelings about marketing.

1. It distracts from my real work. If you only want to be a "technician" solving problems without customer contact, this is correct. If you're a lawyer who only does research, you might survive. If you repair appliances that are received by others, you'll fit your job. But if you repair machines on the shop floor, how you relate to the machine operators—one of your internal customers—is important.

Too Busy for Marketing

Many engineers or inventors love solving problems. But if they haven't talked to potential customers—marketing research—no one may want their solutions. One indication that this is a common problem is the fact that about 95 percent of all patents issued are never brought to the market. Why not do marketing research and solve problems that people *want* to take care of?

2. Fear of rejection by strangers. Only people directly in sales should face this situation.

> "99 percent of failures come from people who have the habit of making excuses."
> —George Washington Carver

Most business owners should be out there doing some selling to keep in touch with their markets.

But most employees who respond to inquiries shouldn't have to deal with this.

The "answer" to this fear is very similar to the:

3. Fear of imposing on others. If you're not imposing and prospects say no, it's not rejection. If you offer something that is a good value for the right people, some of them will thank you for bringing it to their attention. Those who don't need what you have to offer should be able to say so without your feeling rejected.

If someone comes to your retail counter and asks to see something, then doesn't buy it, it's not a rejection of you. You helped rather than imposed. It's the same thing if you're a dental receptionist or a lawyer. When people come to you and you try to help them, if they "reject" you, it's their personality problem, not yours.

If you're proud of what you do, and do the best job you can, you have a customer service attitude and aren't imposing on others. This leads us to the next fear.

4. The sleazy image of selling. Some people in sales *are* sleazy! There is something like $50 million dollars in telemarketing fraud every year in this country. If you're cheating widows and orphans, this book isn't for you! But if you personally *aren't* sleazy and what you offer is a good value, then why worry about the stereotypes of used car salesmen or fraudulent telemarketers?

Accept Rejection, Then Go On

If you're not being rejected, you're not trying hard enough. Lots of successful people have been rejected, probably more times than you have. Actor Tom Selleck was a contestant on "The Dating Game" several times and was never chosen; Sally Jesse Raphael has been fired two times; Gene Hackman was voted "Least Likely to Succeed" by his graduating class; there was a "Loni Anderson Hate Club" in Loni's 6th grade class; Dustin Hoffman's aunt told him he wasn't handsome enough to be an actor.

Good salespeople look at their jobs as a chance to meet a lot of interesting people in different businesses. Even if you're not in sales, that's a healthy attitude to take about people. And since some of them do business with you, your social life is being subsidized!

Take the example of real estate agents. I've worked with some good ones. The best don't try to sell me anything. They're not sleazy. They use their knowledge of the market to save me time and trouble. They act as consultants. They have my best interests at heart because they know I'm a qualified buyer and will respond to good treatment. Your qualified buyers will too.

5. Pressure to produce results. If you accept responsibility for doing some marketing, then you are expected to perform. If you own your own business, you'd *better* accept responsibility for results!

We all dislike failure. And anytime you set a goal, you risk "failure." Successful people know that there is little real failure for the determined person, only delays or setbacks.

Failure "Causes" Success

Perhaps you've heard the story of the young person who asked the most successful woman she knew how she got so successful.

The answer was, "I have a lot of experience."

"Well, how did you get so much experience?"

The final answer was, "I tried a lot of things and failed a lot until I figured out what worked!"

The same approach applies to marketing. You need to try to fail occasionally. But you don't have to make all the mistakes yourself. You can gain experience vicariously by talking with successful people and by reading this and other similar books.

As W.C. Fields said:
"Life is too short to make all the mistakes yourself."

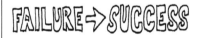

Actually, when things don't go right, you usually learn more about how to achieve your success than when things go right. Plus, you're more motivated to analyze the situation and make changes.

The funny thing is that most of us perform better under a little pressure. Without clear goals and being responsible for results, we often do far less than we can.

SET MARKETING GOALS

If you're the boss, no one else can hold you responsible for results. If you make a clear commitment to marketing efforts, you will achieve two benefits:

The Marketing Mindset

If you do these three things you will be superior in "thinking marketing":

(1) Set aside time to think about how to build relationships with customers and reach new potential customers.

(2) Brainstorm alternative and creative ways to communicate with customers.

(3) Think like the customer. Forget what your organization *sells,* think about what needs customers *want to satisfy* when they buy.

(1) By scheduling marketing as a regular activity, you are more likely to do it and produce results. (And remember, your marketing efforts will be focused on customer service and communication. You probably enjoy talking to customers.)

(2) By setting up marketing procedures and routines, it becomes easier to do marketing—and easier to supervise others doing it for you. (See Chapter 8 for more on the benefits of systems.)

Many of us *need* some pressure to produce results. If you're the boss, you can use a marketing focus as a way to commit yourself to your own success.

It's even better if you make a public commitment to your employees (or spouse) about your marketing efforts. Ask for their help both in holding you accountable and in supporting your efforts. If everyone in your organization sets goals and supports each other, it's easier to sustain a consistent marketing effort. Then you can all share the rewards of each accomplishment.

Rewards for Employees Who Market

If you're an employee whose job title isn't marketing and sales, you can often have the best of both worlds. If you do a good job at your regular work, it may be taken for granted after awhile. But if you do "extra" marketing work, it is very notice-able. It gets attention and sets you apart as someone who is willing to go the extra mile. That's who gets promoted.

Remember, we're not talking cold calls here—unless you like them. What if you organized a seminar or open house for clients? Once you take responsibility, lots of people are willing to help. For instance, you don't have to speak at your seminar; many people would be flattered to be asked. Or perhaps you can add a section to the company Web site, or produce a special report. There are lots of ideas for marketing in the following chap-ters. Pick one and make it "yours."

By keeping your focus on customer relations, everyone benefits. You get better known to cus-tomers and gain internal visibility. Customers feel appreciated and have a chance to communicate their needs and wants. And the company is more successful—and more stable for its employees—by increasing customer loyalty.

The biggest risk for you when you take the responsibility for doing something on marketing is often you're offered a promotion, or a job else-where! Or perhaps you get the entrepreneurial bug when you find out how much fun producing busi-ness can be! Even with a more pessimistic scenario, you can minimize your risks for any marketing initiatives you take so that a good payoff is more likely.

> "More customer service hopes have been wrecked on the rigid shores of immobile bureaucratic minds than anywhere else."
> —Ken Blanchard and Sheldon Bowles, *Raving Fans*

A CUSTOMER SERVICE/MARKETING ATTITUDE

The Marketing Concept

For twenty years, marketing textbooks have been talking about "the marketing concept." This says that organizations (profit and nonprofit) should:

- focus on consumer needs
- design the organization to satisfy these needs
- achieve profits (or results for nonprofits) through satisfying needs, including the needs of society

The marketing concept says that organizations should analyze the needs of potential customers and then make decisions about how to satisfy them. Marketing is not about forcing things on people. It should create value for customers.

Somehow, this constructive marketing concept is not being translated into day-to-day marketing activities by most people. But we hope this book will help you and your organization take such a customer-focused approach to marketing.

Approval to Say "No"

At L.L. Bean, before any employee can say "no" to a customer, he or she has to have senior management approval.

At McMurry Publishing, the only acceptable answers to a customer request is, "Yes, we can..." and "Yes, we will..." They worry later about what that "yes" will cost. President Preston McMurry believes that it's not the "yes" decisions that kill a company, but the "no" decisions.

—*Executive Edge* newsletter

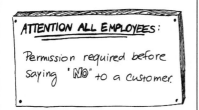

ATTENTION ALL EMPLOYEES:
Permission required before saying "NO" to a customer.

Business is 1-1

I like the rule that a few radical companies use in their interactions with customers. Employees have to get permission to say "no" to a customer!

That's right. It's the opposite of most companies' procedures where employees have to get permission to do anything, let alone anything out of the ordinary to take initiatives to help customers!

As the Mafia "Godfather" said in the movie, "All business is personal." No matter how big your organization, customers deal with people. While ongoing business relationships can involve electronic data interchange, the Internet, or automatic tellers, it's the people connections that build loyalty. Remembering someone's name, or sharing their interests is more powerful than an expensive brochure or advertisement.

Anybody who comes into contact with customers contributes to the most powerful marketing available. Customers form impressions of you from each contact, whether you're ready or not. And they give you word-of-mouth whether you want it or not. How you treat them will determine if it is good or bad.

Internal Customer Service

Anyone who supports the people who come into contact with customers can also make a difference. People in the warehouse can get shipments out early to thrill customers. People in accounting can handle problems better, and so forth.

For instance, recently a plastic parts distributor in Portland needed an overnight shipment from WestEdge in San Francisco, but UPS had already left. The warehouse manager for WestEdge told the customer service rep that the UPS truck would be driving past again at the end of the route. He offered to flag the truck down to get a late shipment out. The customer was thrilled by the "can do" attitude.

> ### Serving Internal Customers
>
> To better serve internal customers:
> - let internal customers rate the people who should serve them
> - hold department managers responsible for cross-department coordination
> - cross-train employees so they'll understand others' jobs and be able to pitch in
>
> —Ken Blanchard, Blanchard Training and Development

Promises Fulfilled

There's another subtle but very important issue involving internal customer service. How your internal support people behave will affect the confidence customer contact people have in making promises.

For instance, if your organization is bureaucratic where people care more about protecting their backsides than taking care of customers, customer service will be weaker. Having to deal with jerks inside your organization will make people grumpier in dealing with customers. That's a major point in Hal Rosenbluth's book, *The Customer Comes Second.* Your people treat customers about as well as they're treated!

Internal Conflict about Marketing

In companies large enough to have departments, it's not unusual for there to be conflict between them. Customer service or engineering say that the salespeople are making promises that no customer service or technology could live up to. The salespeople say that customer service is the problem or that the engineers design products nobody wants and nobody could sell.

People go into different types of work because they have different skills and interests. This creates personality, communication, and other conflicts.

An example of "war" between departments about marketing occurred during a brainstorming session in a customer service department. The problem was that salespeople were making promises they couldn't fulfill. The first solution the customer service group envisioned was to attack the sales department. Instead, the group explored how they could cooperate with sales to better serve customers, and came up with an action plan.

Break Down Department Walls

Here's an example of how an interdepartmental communication breakdown can affect customers—and profits.

The marketing department of a large company arranged a major television commercial on a local football broadcast. The commercial gave an 800 number to call for information. Sounds good, so far...

But the first that anyone in the customer service department heard about it was when the vice president saw the commercial at home. Nobody was covering the phones during the weekend broadcast!

CALL
1-800-
NO
ANSWER

Getting Together for Results

Customer service approached sales with an offer to try to help them make more money by improving repeat business. They suggested that sales was spending too much time looking for new business and not enough time serving current customers and getting referrals.

Eventually, the managers of sales and customer service made a joint proposal to the president to suspend sales quotas for six months while the two groups concentrated on repeat and referral business. Within two years, *net sales rose 40 percent* and *employee turnover in customer service dropped by 25 percent*. Both of these are very profitable trends!

When everyone in your organization realizes that marketing is all about customer service, it can pull an organization together. In a successful organization, everyone enjoys working both with customers *and* with each other.

Really Turn the Pyramid Upside Down

There's a lot of talk about customer focus, but not much action. To set the tone for a true customer-focused organization, support must come from the top. But the image of top-down leadership for customer service isn't the right metaphor to get it done.

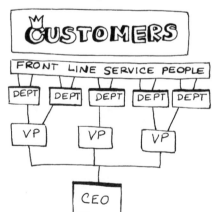

In the old corporate pyramid, the CEO is at the top, and the customer contact people at the bottom. This puts customers "below" everyone in the company.

While it's true that customers provide the foundation for any organization, it's better if you turn the pyramid over and put the customer on top. That puts the CEO at the bottom. While lots of CEOs talk about serving customers, few put themselves in the right position to support everyone else in the company who directly serves customers!

> "If you're looking up at me [the boss], you've got your ass pointed at the customer."
> —Jack Welch, General Electric

SUMMARY

The reasons marketing is for everyone who wants to succeed are many. If you own a business, without customers there is no business. If you're an employee, you will be worth more to your employer, and you'll increase your own options, if you deal well with internal and external customers. You'll also enjoy your work more when you enjoy people—and customers *are* people!

I've suggested why marketing can be positive instead of negative for you. And many cases in the following chapters provide more examples. To improve your organization, improve your marketing. That doesn't mean to sell in a "slicker" way. That means to involve all your people in better serving customers.

Marketing 101

Marketing is defined as anything you do to get *or* keep customers. We know that most successful organizations have from 60 to 90 percent repeat business.

> "Business is built on the loyal customer, one who comes back and brings a friend."
> —W. Edwards Deming

Customer relationships built through superior service are the first key to success.

The second key is to cultivate referrals from the base of customers and others who know you.

This has little in common with most people's images of what marketing involves.

Your Best Marketers

Your biggest source of marketing results—repeat business—is probably employees whose job titles are *not* in marketing and sales. How they treat customers and prospects can make all the difference.

Every person who answers your phones, greets customers, and contacts customers is key. Yet how many employees make customers happy they purchased from you? When I ask in my seminars, people have a dozen stories of bad customer service for every great one.

I'm not blaming employees. They're often untrained and unrewarded for making sure customers have a satisfying experience with the company. This may reflect how uncomfortable the owners of businesses are about marketing.

Action Counts

To move forward, you need to build marketing into your behavior. The first secret to getting this done is to test different things you can do to see what works and is comfortable for you. Match your style to your customers. The subsequent chapters give you lots of marketing techniques to experiment with.

MARKETING ACTION PLAN

(1) Test different marketing activities
(2) Get started
(3) Set up a routine

How Well Do We Know Our Customers?

by Peter Drucker

What the people in the business think they know about the customer and market is more likely to be wrong than right. There is only one person who really knows: the customer. Only by asking the customer, by watching him, by trying to understand his behavior can one find out who he is, what he does, how he buys, how he uses what he buys, what he expects, what he values, and so on.

The customer rarely buys what the business thinks it sells him. One reason for this is, of course, that nobody pays for a "product." What is paid for is satisfactions. But nobody can make or supply satisfactions as such—at best, only the means to attaining them can be sold and delivered.

Because the customer buys satisfaction, all goods and services compete intensively with goods and services that look quite different, seem to serve entirely different functions, are made, distributed, sold differently—but are alternatives means for the customer to obtain the same satisfaction.

The second secret is to get going. It's better to try something and learn from setbacks than to do nothing. All the chapters have action-oriented summaries.

The third secret is to build marketing into your regular routine. This could be always sending thank-you notes, giving talks, or answering the phone by the second ring.

Routines make it easier to do great marketing. The last two chapters focus on the value of systematic marketing programs and how to implement one for yourself or your organization.

Whatever your position, getting closer to customers will help you. Try it, you'll like it!

ACTION SUMMARY

"An unsown seed bears nothing."
—Japanese proverb

Even if marketing is not your main job, there are seeds you can sow now to reap extra rewards.

1 Write down what you don't like about marketing and how you might overcome each mental block.

2 Write down what you like about marketing. Figure out how you can do more and enjoy marketing more.

3 Hold a meeting to discuss how all employees can become involved in thrilling customers.

4 Brainstorm new ways to be in regular touch with customers.

5 Do a quick survey of customers to get ideas of their interests.

6 If you have departments in conflict, hold a joint meeting to focus everyone on customer needs.

7 Set up rewards to share profits with everyone who contributes to generating new or repeat business (include the internal support people).

8 Consider offering incentives to nonmarketing employees and salespeople who support customers or sales (see Chapter 7).

9 Decide how you can give better service to current customers.

10 Decide how you can reward employees (or yourself) for better serving customers.

11 List ways the CEO can support people who serve customers.

12 If you're the boss, decide how you can support and better reward internal customer service.

13 Redefine your "work" to include a regular customer service/marketing component.

14 Pick a regular time every day to contact customers, or do some other marketing task.

15 Design marketing research that will tell you more about what your customers want—for instance, talk to them, do a survey, or ask your frontline employees for suggestions.

16 Commit to reading books such as this to give you more ideas to put into practice.

Chapter 2

USING MARKETING TO BUILD A SUCCESSFUL BUSINESS

Jim Rhode

Jim Rhode, BME, CSP, chairman of SmartPractice, has developed and presented hundreds of seminars and workshops on practice administration and professional marketing for three decades. He has spoken to thousands of progressive dentists, and their spouses and staff members.

From his years in industry as a long-range planner with American Can Company and Celanese Corporation, Mr. Rhode brings to the healthcare profession scores of practice-building techniques and the motivation for timely implementation. His extensive business experience includes team building, financial analysis, operation streamlining, and long-range planning.

He is a member of the National Speakers Association and the Business Mailers Group. Mr. Rhode was honored with the prestigious Arizona Entrepreneur of the Year award for 1990. He has given talks in all 50 states, and 13 foreign countries. In addition, he is the publisher of *PracticeSmart: Dentistry's Marketing and Management Newsletter*.

Jim's philosophy is best summarized by the proverb: "Any enterprise is built by wise planning...becomes strong through common sense...and profits wonderfully by keeping abreast of the facts."

Jim Rhode, SmartPractice, 3400 East McDowell, Phoenix, AZ 85008-7899; phone (602) 225-9090; fax (602) 225-0599.

Chapter 2

USING MARKETING TO BUILD A SUCCESSFUL BUSINESS

Jim Rhode

"There is only one boss: the customer. And he can fire everybody in the company, from the chairman on down, simply by spending his money somewhere else."
—Sam Walton, founder, Wal-Mart

If your business is like most, chances are your customers are suffering from a serious syndrome that can zap your business' growth. It's called the *"out-of-sight, out-of-mind syndrome."*

Even the most satisfied clients can forget about the quality services you offer. So, the next time they need what you offer, they *may* call you. Or, they may call a competitor who just sent them an introductory offer in the mail or who was just referred by a friend. This cuts you out of that all-important repeat business which should account for at least 60 percent of your business, and 80 percent of your profits!

If your clients are suffering from this syndrome, they are also less likely to refer others to you who need your services. Referrals should account for at least 20 percent of your business, the majority of your new business, and the rest of your profits!

So, how do you overcome this *out-of-sight, out-of-mind syndrome*? How do you keep the repeat business you deserve? How do you build referrals? How do you involve your staff in creating a more successful business?

This chapter will help you get started on setting up a system for a profitable business based on repeat business and referrals. The chapters that follow this one will give you more material on which to build your success.

I work largely with service providers who own a practice, so that's what I'll discuss. However, the same principles apply to retailing and manufacturing. And, for a program to be successful, employees must be supportive participants.

THREE POSSIBILITIES FOR EVERY BUSINESS OWNER

To be really successful as a business owner or professional, you first must make a decision and then a commitment to follow up on your decision. Setting up a successful business requires an investment in *marketing*. You may wonder: "Do I really have to make such an investment?" Well, consider your options:

1. Get a job with another professional who is a great marketer. In the past 10 years, many physicians have done just that. Most doctors once were freestanding independents who managed

Lifetime Value

It's important to know the expected lifetime value of a customer. For the income side, this means you need to know:

- how long the average customer stays
- how much they purchase

Then add the value of expected referrals.

On the cost side, calculate:

- acquisition costs, and
- your costs to meet their needs.

You can do precise estimates discounting future expected revenues to current dollar values, or you can do rough calculations. Either way, you should be impressed by how much a happy, repeat customer can be worth to you over time. (See also Chapter 6.)

and marketed their own practices. Today, many (or should I say most) have gone to work for large clinics or HMOs. Almost all of the new medical school graduates have launched their careers this way. Such a move frees you from marketing responsibilities, but at a price. Generally speaking, going to work for an employer who does the marketing reduces your "income opportunities" by 50 percent.

2. Locate your business or practice in a small or rural community. In small communities, the supply and demand factor is often in favor of the professional person. In many cases, you are the lone provider or supplier of your service. The downside is there may not be a market large enough to fill your schedule. Also, the availability of staff with proper credentials may be limited. This can be overcome with a substantial commitment and budget.

3. Make the decision to market your services. Yes, this means developing a real marketing plan with strategy, goals, and action plan (see Chapters 8 and 9 for more details).

The 1950s' economy was one of scarcity—with a shortage of services. Today, we're in the midst of a glut economy—there's a serious oversupply of most products and services. For example, it's estimated that within five years there will be more than a million lawyers in the United States. Roughly 70 percent of all lawyers on the planet will be plying their trade in the U.S.

There's also bad news for doctors. Studies

have estimated that there could be an excess of approximately 165,000 specialists by the turn of the century. Similarly, the nation is stocked with too many consultants and accountants.

To ensure that you will have plenty of customers, the solution is effective marketing. Certainly, marketing means an expenditure of time and money. But you must remember new clients typically become repeat customers; thus, they have a significant *lifetime value.* You can amortize your marketing costs for them over multiple purchases or multiple service cycles.

THE THREE "ANGLES" OF A SUCCESSFUL, GROWING, HEALTHY BUSINESS

Basic wisdom from management gurus like Peter Drucker says that any business consists of three parts: getting the business, doing the work, and accounting for the business. These are marketing, delivery of the service or product, and administrative and paperwork systems.

The triangle to the right portrays these three general functions in the order that corresponds to the amount of attention you need to pay to them. I also assume that you know your business well and you love what you do. Without these factors, you really can't succeed.

2
GETTING
CUSTOMERS

SUCCESS
TRIANGLE

1
PERFORMANCE

3
MANAGEMENT

1. Do a Great Job

The first angle of the triangle is to perform all the tasks tied to your business. If you don't do a great job, no marketing or system can make you successful. If you're a physician, dentist, or veterinarian, that means diagnosing illnesses, recommending treatments, and training staff. If you're an accountant, that means performing financial analysis, preparing documents, and training para-professionals. If you're a lawyer, that means investigating complaints, interviewing the parties involved, and applying cases to the law. If you're a financial advisor, that means interviewing your clients, evaluating their incomes and expenses, and developing financial plans that will achieve their goals.

Giving good service is something that owners and staff should all be able to agree upon. There is a dignity in great service that too many people don't appreciate.

> "There is intrinsic security that comes from service, from helping other people in a meaningful way."
> —Stephen Covey

2. Market Effectively

The second angle is getting customers, patients, or clients. In most fields, there no longer is an unlimited supply of clients. It's no longer enough to simply do a great job. There are a growing number of competitors going after your customers and prospects. At the least, you have to remind your clients to come in again, and to give you referrals.

This book will help you feel more comfortable with marketing, even if marketing functions are not included in your job description. With competition becoming keener in your field, you need to help produce repeat business, referrals, and sufficient new clients, new patients, or new customers to fill your schedule—and to achieve your business goals. That's what marketing is all about.

3. Manage Better

The third and final angle of this success model is management. Effective management means organizing your business for both the short and long term. In the short term, if it's your business, systems help take care of the routine work and establish quality that delivers better service to customers. If you're an employee, systems let you know what is expected, and free up your creativity for beyond-the-call-of-duty service and new projects.

In the long term, managing your business means making the dollar numbers work for you! What good is it to be the best there is in your profession—and get all the clients there are if—at the end of your working life, you have nothing to show for it? This requires budgeting—both in the present and for your future. Employee 401K plans or profit sharing can create staff stability that serves customers and clients even better. Participation in such tax-deferred plans allows you to cash in on the magic of compound interest. (It's only after you've seen your savings or mutual fund double that you really appreciate the magic of compound interest.)

ENCOURAGING REPEAT BUSINESS

As already mentioned, 60 percent or more of your business, and 80 percent or more of your profits will probably come from repeat business. The necessity of taking good care of your current customers is why everyone is in marketing, whether they think about it or not.

Of course, the first thing you have to do to earn repeat business is to do a good job at what you do. But to really win loyalty, you need to go further. You need to thrill customers, to exceed their expectations, or to establish a personal emotional bond. This is where most businesses fall down.

How to Create Raving Fans

(1) Determine what you love to do.

(2) Discover what the customer wants from you.

(3) Deliver, plus one percent.

— Ken Blanchard and Sheldon Bowles, *Raving Fans*

Giveaways Stay in Their Minds

Besides great service, what other methods can you use to encourage repeat business? One way is to keep your business name, logo, phone number, and concept in front of your clients in between business contacts. One of the easiest ways to do this is with cost-effective, personalized giveaways that your customers will associate with you.

Useful items such as personalized mugs filled with flowers or jelly beans delivered to customers' workplaces, or personalized calendars, key rings, and magnets are all great ways to keep your name in front of people. If you want to see this principle in action, just go to a doctor's office. You'll find pens, notepads, and posters imprinted with the logos of pharmaceutical companies. These items make it more likely that the drug company's name will be right in front of the physician when he or she has the occasion to write a prescription for medication.

Here's how the magic of personalized giveaways can work for you. First, identify where clients are most likely to think about you or need your services or products. Then tie your name to that place or event—just like the pharmaceutical companies have done in physicians' treatment rooms.

For example, let's say you're a dentist who has identified new teachers as a good market. You send a thank-you gift of flowers in a mug imprinted with your name, logo, and phone number to a patient who is a teacher at a nearby school. The

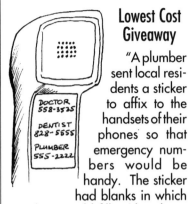

Lowest Cost Giveaway

"A plumber sent local residents a sticker to affix to the handsets of their phones so that emergency numbers would be handy. The sticker had blanks in which residents could fill in the phone numbers of their doctors, dentists, and the emergency room. Of course, in the event that a resident has a plumbing emergency, the plumber's phone number was imprinted on the sticker. His company name was seen every time a resident used the phone."

—Rick Crandall, *Marketing Your Services: For People Who Hate to Sell* eye-catching mug and flowers are placed on a table in the teacher's lounge, where the entire faculty can't help but notice your name and logo. During a coffee break, the topic of conversation turns to you. "My dentist is very gentle and takes time to explain things to me," your patient tells two new teachers in the lounge who don't yet have a dentist. Three other teachers—who are disgruntled because their dentists *never* explain things—overhear the conversation. They quickly decide you're the one they'll call for their next cleaning and check-up. The same concept works for veterinarians, mechanics, and others.

Keep Good Records to Keep in Touch

Keeping your name in front of clients is an easier task than ever today, thanks to the vast array of affordable personal computers and database software on the market. You can use this technology to maintain a customer database with the names, addresses, and phone numbers of all the clients you've served.

MAILING FOR SUCCESS

To eliminate the *out-of-sight, out-of-mind syndrome*, use your database to send your customers at least four communications—newsletters, announcements, holiday greetings, etc.—per year. It doesn't matter whether or not customers and prospects read your material word for word. Just a brief glimpse of your name and logo has a powerful effect. Businesses

Do You Know Your Customers?

Harvey Mackay, envelope manufacturer and author of *Swim with the Sharks...*, requires his salespeople to collect 66 items of information about prospects and clients. Information includes birthdays, children, where customers went to school, hobbies, where they like to eat, and so forth. You can't build relationships with people if you don't know anything about them!

CUSTOMER INFO

BIRTHDAY _____

CHILDREN _____

HOBBIES _____

FAVORITE RESTAURANTS

report a burst of new work after each mailing that usually covers the mailing costs.

Regular mailings can also be used to build a new business. For instance, to make ends meet, one service provider in a small town had to commute two hours several days a week in order to work in another professional's office. After she started doing a simple mailing to local people, she built up her own practice so she could stay in town. Most new clients who came to her as a result of these mailings said they hadn't even known she was in town. She had to do the mailings to become an "in-sight" provider.

Mailing Is Most Effective

The powerful impact of mailings is documented in the first-ever Gallup Organization Direct Mail Study. The recent study showed that marketing executives consider direct mail to be the most effective technique in achieving six out of seven critical marketing objectives, including:

- generating sales
- cost effectiveness
- educating consumers about complex issues
- selling products directly to households or businesses
- informing consumers or businesses about new products or services
- tracking results and effectiveness

Only in the case of "increasing brand identity" was direct mail ranked behind magazines, TV, and newspapers.

What to Mail

You may be wondering: "What could I send my clients that would deliver the most bang for the buck?" Be creative. Marketing genius Harvey Mackay recommends sending Thanksgiving cards. Unlike Christmas cards that stuff mailboxes during the holiday season, Thanksgiving cards are seldom sent. So chances are, your card might be the only one your client receives. Also, Thanksgiving cards can include heartwarming messages—how much you appreciate your client, how *thankful* you are for the opportunity to serve them, or how important your client is to you.

The first rule of mailing is to set up a program to do *something*. Most people just never get around to getting started. The second rule is to stay in regular contact. The third rule is to be personal and creative. A newsletter is okay, but a personal clipping and note is better.

REASONS TO BE IN TOUCH

Here are some ways you can expand your potential communications with customers and prospects and build your business at the same time:

Announce:
- your business' new technology or techniques that can better serve clients
- new staff members
- a new associate or partner
- a new service, such as extended, client-pleasing hours
- moving to a new location (mail twice; four weeks before the move and two weeks afterward)

Thank you:
- for a referral

Welcome:
- new clients
- new neighbors

Invitation:
- open house or special event you are hosting

Community service:
- "after the flood," please call to reschedule

Many of these reasons for being in touch with your customers are also useful for publicity. When something happens in your business, you can use it as the basis for a brief press release to the media.

Mailings by the Calendar

You can also tie your mailings to the seasons:

- a "what's new" announcement after January 1
- a St. Patrick's Day "We're Lucky to Have You for a Customer" card or postcard
- a birthday card tied to the birthday of someone famous in your field (for example, Abraham Lincoln for lawyers, Charles Lindbergh for travel agents)
- a summer schedule in May
- an Independence Day card to clients of financial planners congratulating them on working towards financial independence
- a card tied to the many national days, weeks, and months (Heart Month in February for doctors, Save Your Vision Week in March for optometrists and ophthalmologists, Foot Health Month in August for podiatrists, Customer Service Week in October for any business, Computer Security Day in November for computer consultants, and so forth)
- if your business has seasonal ups and downs, a special offer tied to your slow season
- a Friendship Day card in August
- a card with the local football team's schedule in the fall
- a Halloween card—either alone or with a special offer ("It's no trick, we'd like to treat you to..." a 10% off coupon, a free report, free coffee and cookies Halloween week)

More Reasons to Write

Here are some more reasons for you to be in touch with customers (from the book *Marketing Magic*):

- to make an appointment
- to apologize
- for an anniversary—theirs personally, or their anniversary of becoming your customer
- following a phone contact
- after a purchase
- a "we miss you" note
- congratulations on their personal achievements
- a social invitation

The important thing is to make it easy to send a note. Have a system and the materials in place so notes are automatically triggered on a regular basis.

WORD-OF-MOUTH MARKETING

The second most important form of marketing is referrals. Word-of-mouth marketing can overcome the *out-of-sight, out-of-mind syndrome.* This is the most cost-effective way a business can grow new customers. The basis of word-of-mouth marketing is creating experiences that will keep others talking about you.

Let's say you had dinner last night at a fabulous new restaurant. A co-worker stops you in the breakroom and asks, "I'm looking for a good place to take my friend to dinner—do you have a suggestion?" You say, "Yes, try the new restaurant. The food's great, and the service is prompt." Your positive influence or recommendation—a word-of-mouth endorsement of the restaurant—has just significantly influenced your co-worker's dining decision. That's an example of the positive influence of word-of-mouth.

Negative Word-of-Mouth

Unfortunately, it's the negative talk that reaches a much wider audience. According to Jerry R. Wilson, author of *Word-of-Mouth Marketing,* for every three people willing to tell a positive story about an experience with your company, there are 33 others who will tell a horror story. This quirk in human nature makes it obvious that the number one marketing rule already mentioned under repeat business applies here, too. You must be offering good products or services. You can be sure that customers of businesses with bad products or services are out there spreading bad news—and you know that nothing makes a business fail faster!

Control Your Marketing Climate

This powerful marketing force of word-of-mouth is like the weather. Many professionals feel powerless to change it. But you *can* transform a customer's rave reviews into referrals and increased repeat business. And, you can transform unhappy customers into fans by taking care of their problems on the spot (see Chapter 4).

Be Your Own Cause

"Evangelism is the process of selling a dream. Selling a dream means transforming a vision into a cause and getting people to share that cause. Thus, evangelism is the purest form of selling....When people believe in your cause, they sustain it during difficult times and against all comers....Evangelism makes a cause snowball as more people adopt the same beliefs."

—Guy Kawasaki, *Selling the Dream*

Turning your satisfied customers into unpaid marketing evangelists is the most cost-effective way to build sales over the long term. Sure, you can buy short-term sales "spikes" through radio, newspaper, and television advertising—but at what cost? In most communities, 80 percent of media advertising is wasted on consumers who will never, or rarely, be paying customers because they live or work too far away from the advertised business.

MARKETING IS EVERYONE'S JOB

Since effective marketing consists largely of encouraging repeat business and referrals, I think it is clear that staff members whose jobs are not officially marketing and sales can be the most important marketers. For instance, in doctors' offices, receptionists, nurses, and assistants usually have more contact with clients than the doctors. These employees need to look for ways to build relationships, thrill clients, and ask verbally or nonverbally for referrals.

Hopefully, reading this book will be a good start on involving your staff in marketing. Here are some ideas you can discuss with your staff on how they can be involved in improving your marketing program.

7 Practice-Growth Questions for Staff Discussion

1. What type of poster, chart, graph, or schedule of events (such as sports) could our office imprint with our name, logo, and phone number to give to our clients?

2. What activities or actions can we as a team make to support a word-of-mouth marketing agenda? How can staff members be comfortable asking for referrals? What can we give out for clients to pass on to others? (For instance, accountants can give out extra tax planners to their clients to pass on to an associate or neighbor.)

3. How can we provide specific, exceptional, repeatable service to our clients to create positive experiences that will feed word-of-mouth marketing?

4. How can we thank or reward clients who've referred new business to encourage them to do so again? What kind and value of gift is appropriate and indicated?

5. What types of communications—such as announcements, newsletters, and greeting cards—could we send out to our clients on a quarterly basis?

6. How can we cut the cycle time or waiting time for the primary service we offer?

7. Because it may be impossible to please all of the people all of the time, how can we "diffuse" dissatisfied customers to stop the spread of negative word-of-mouth?

CONCLUSION

The following chapters in this book go into more details on how to build a successful marketing program, whether you're an owner or employee. Three basic principles were covered in this chapter.

First, realize that taking good care of your existing customers is by far the most important marketing you can do. Unless you're new, repeat business should account for 60–80 percent of your business, or even more.

> "Quality in a service or product is not what you put into it. It is what the client or customer gets out of it."
>
> —Peter Drucker

Second, generating good word-of-mouth and referrals is the best way to obtain new clients. People give you word-of-mouth whether you want it or not. Shouldn't you have a program designed to "knock their socks off" so the word-of-mouth will be great?

Third, it takes everyone in the business to make the first two principles work. Employees must be involved in delivering great service and creating word-of-mouth. If they don't believe in the value of what you offer, why should customers? Select, train, and reward employees for their contributions to the success of the business. Technical skills are not enough. Everyone must treat your customers like "kings" so you can all succeed.

ACTION AGENDA

> "Great works are performed not by strength, but perseverance."
>
> —Samuel Johnson

Now that you've had a glimpse of the big picture, it's time to set goals. Here are eight that will boost your business:

1 Since you now know the importance of keeping your name and logo in front of clients—and effective ways to do it—send at least four mailings per year to every active account.

2 Identify your key repeat and new business ingredients. Good business practice dictates that this number be recorded on a monthly basis. The goal should be 120 to 150 percent of last year's business for the same month.

3 Cut the cycle time or waiting time for the primary service that you do. The photo development industry is a prime example. Photo development used to take a week.

Later, it took three days. More recently, one-hour photo development services sprang up everywhere. And now, some services have sliced processing time down to 30 minutes. For your business, set the goal to cut your lead time, delivery time, or client waiting time in half—or whatever is reasonable for you. Push yourself on this one. New technology—especially computers—can make it happen. Cutting your time will give you and your office a competitive edge (and something positive for your clients to talk about).

4 Identify—with help from your staff and associates—potential new clients or referral sources. Set a goal to make at least 10 contacts per month with these potential clients or referral sources—preferably at a breakfast, lunch or dinner meeting. For example, if an orthodontist sets and achieves this goal, he/she might have three breakfasts, six lunches, and one dinner per month with dentists in the area who could or would refer patients.

5 Identify key time-consuming tasks you have always performed that could or should be transferred to a staff member. Empower your staff to do more so that you can do more of what only you can do.

6 Decide as a team to refer more business to other professionals who could or should refer business to your office. Follow up each referral with a telephone call to the professional to let him/her know you are sending new business. A good goal would be two outbound referrals per month for each staff member. Assign one person the task of keeping a referral list, managing this goal, and reporting back to you.

7 Next, fill in the blank, or set your own goal specific to your profession: _____

8 Set a specific schedule that includes dates, responsibility (with staff names), and time to achieve the seven business-building goals above.

Chapter 3

THE SECRETS OF EFFECTIVE NETWORKING

Elaine C. Dumler

Elaine C. Dumler
is a professional speaker and
consultant. As co-owner of
Frankly Speaking... she has
provided presentation and communication skill programs nationwide to corporate clients including General Electric, Mobil Chemical, Johnson & Johnson, and State Farm Insurance. Her expertise in building businesses through referrals has helped to advance the relationship marketing skills of representatives from Shaklee, Mary Kay Cosmetics, Pampered Chef, Excel Telecommunications, and other direct marketing companies.

As a former chapter consultant for a Leads Club, Ms. Dumler understands the presentation and networking needs of business people. For eight years, she worked with their chapter members helping them learn to use networking techniques as a profitable marketing tool. Her clients' successes have led to the development of her programs, "BIG Results from small talk!," and "Put Your Mouth Where the Money Is." She has written several articles on networking and public speaking, and has appeared as a guest on both radio and television.

Ms. Dumler is a member of the Colorado chapter of the National Speakers Association and has served on their board of directors and as chairperson of the mentor/protégé program.

Elaine C. Dumler, Frankly Speaking, 1244 Ceres Drive, Lafayette, CO 80026; phone (303) 665-5319; fax (303) 665-1280; e-mail FraklySpkg@aol.com.

Chapter 3

THE SECRETS OF EFFECTIVE NETWORKING

Elaine C. Dumler

"Up the proverbial creek? If you've got a network, you've always got a paddle."
—Harvey Mackay, *Dig Your Well Before You're Thirsty*

Networking is making connections with other people for the mutually beneficial exchange of ideas, information, and contacts. Most people think of networking as telling everyone you meet exactly what *you* want. But even more important is finding out what *others* want—and helping them get it!

NETWORKING IS A PHILOSOPHY

I enjoy being known as a resource for others. It's satisfying to watch someone get what they need. As a networker, I am often approached with the question, "Do you know someone who can help me...?" Most of the time I do. Making that connection allows us to talk further and they, in turn, may discover that they know someone who can help me! What goes around, comes around.

NETWORKING REQUIRES ACTION

Networking is an action word. You have to get out there and interact. Don't just sit on the sidelines waiting for people to come to you. Go ahead and make the first move to meet someone. You never know where that connection will lead you. It's a common notion that the person who can get you what you want is just a few contacts away from you right now! That's exciting! Your job is to define what your networking goals are and to reach out to find your key contacts.

> Luck is preparation meeting opportunity, and the way to let your preparation meet opportunities is to network.

Networking has been called "the business tool of the '90s." As the '90s come to a close, and the next millennium is upon us, we see technology advancing at a phenomenal pace. Technological progress tends to separate people. Yet we have an instinct for personal human contact.

We need to connect with people. As our contact time with each other grows less and less, we need to be sure we are making the most of every moment we have. Your people skills need to be topnotch. Research has shown that 85 percent of your success on a job is due to your people skills. Your technical knowledge only accounts for 15 percent of your success! So, networking isn't such a small skill after all!

Fewer Than "Six Degrees of Separation"

In the '60s, psychologist Stanley Milgram did an experiment to see how many intermediaries separated any two people in the United States. For example, if your goal were to reach the president of General Motors, you would call someone you knew on a first-name basis. That person would then talk to someone they knew, and so forth. For those who tried, the median length chain connecting any two people was five.

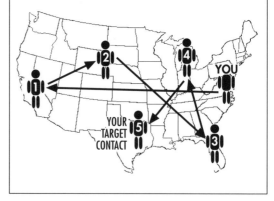

HOW NETWORKING BUILDS SUCCESS

Opportunities to network present themselves dozens of times each day. Better networking will improve your business and your life.

Better Contacts

If you're networking for business, the contacts you make through networking are of high quality. Networking is one of the best ways to stay informed. If you are a part of a large company, it's important to know what is going on and how the part you play affects the organization. Networking allows you to do this. Your informal connections help you do your job better and get ahead.

Online Networking

Technology can improve your networking. Today you can spend hours "talking" with someone over the Internet and never meet face to face. Many virtual companies, friendships, and referrals have come as a result of e-mail and other technologies.

Job Leads

Are you job hunting? The people around you are a rich source of "hidden" job opportunities and employment leads. As you are looking for a new position, acquaint yourself with professionals in your field. They often know where the prime jobs are and can open doors for you when you might otherwise be left out.

More Referrals

Referrals supplied by your networking contacts are some of your best new business leads. For example, asking for a referral from a satisfied client is an easy, natural thing to do. Yet few people take that step. In a survey done for the *Edward Jones Investment Newsletter*, it was found that "86 percent of investors who work with investment representatives said they would recommend that person to other investors yet only 12 percent said their representative had ever asked them for a referral." How sad—a lot of business is being missed.

SET NETWORKING GOALS

We set goals in many other aspects of our lives. It's no different with networking. Your networking goals will change as your needs change. If you are in the job market, your current goal will be to find a good job appropriate for your skills. When you have landed a job, new goals will take its place. Network to learn more about your company, your industry, and the role you can play in both.

Maybe, right now, your networking goal is of a more personal nature. Networking is the best way to find a quality real estate or insurance agent, an accountant, a doctor, dentist, or babysitter.

> ## Networking Is Fun!
> The best networking comes naturally. Networking often takes place at leisure activities in which you participate. It's fun to meet others and to discover how you can help them. In turn, you usually find that you get what you're looking for, too!

If you are in business for yourself, your goals should be more specific. Would you like a certain number of new clients? Determine how many people you need to talk with who can lead you to the new business. Where do you enjoy networking? Be sure to put yourself in those situations at least three times a week. Do you need information and research data for a book or article you are writing? Set a goal to search out those who can lead you to the best sources.

Set Goals "Backwards"

I find that I need to work backwards from my desired results to set the best goals. For instance, to get one speaking engagement, I need to talk with at least 10 people. From these 10, four will usually be able to refer me to someone who they believe has a need for my services. One speaking opportunity should result from my follow-up with the four contacts. You can see that to book three jobs, I should set a goal of letting 30 people know what I do. Then I need to find those 30 people.

WHERE DO PEOPLE NETWORK?

A networking opportunity can present itself wherever you find someone to talk to. The most obvious places are those events designed for networking. These could include chamber of commerce functions, business mixers, events sponsored by professional associations, and networking club meetings. And don't forget the "breaks" at seminars, workshops, and conferences.

> ### Networking at Conventions and Conferences
>
> Conferences, seminars, and conventions are great for networking. Use the time wisely that you have between sessions, at meals, trade fairs, and in the evenings.
>
>

Other places to network may not be quite so obvious. Some of my favorites include the recreation center, parties and informal dinners, the coffee hour following church, and all the activities in which my children are involved.

Out of all the people I meet in these places, who will care about "my story?" Let's delve a little deeper into defining the people who will be instrumental to the success of your networking.

DEVELOPING YOUR PEOPLE RESOURCES AND CENTERS OF INFLUENCE

Networking involves sharing your goals with as many people as possible. We need to determine who these people are, where to find them, and how to see if we can help each other. Statistics say we each know at least 250 other people. Let's take a moment to go through an exercise that will help you know specifically whom to call on when you need information or help. This network of people will serve as a source for new projects and current activities.

Look at where you spend your time. Where do you meet the people who are a part of your life?

Mentally, take yourself through a typical day. After you wake up and get dressed, where do you go? Do you head out for the *gym*, or go directly to *work*? During your work day, do you attend any *professional association meetings*, or related activities such as Toastmasters? After dinner, do you usually spend time at home with your family or do you occasionally attend an *evening activity*? What about the time you spend at your *children's events and programs*? Sometimes you can spend more time talking with the person sitting next to you on the bleachers at your son's baseball game than you do with the person at the desk next to you at work. Go through your calendar for the previous month and note what *professional appointments* you had and whom they were with. Did you see your accountant, your doctor, or your dentist? These are all people with whom you can network.

ANALYZE YOUR CONTACTS

On the worksheet on the following page, in each numbered space, write one of the areas in where you meet people. See if you can fill all eight spaces, describing them in a very general manner.

Some of the categories in my life include: my church or spiritual life, recreation and fitness, family, close friends, people at work, each professional association I am involved with, my children's activities, those individuals with whom I do business (doctor, dentist, insurance agent, my own clients, etc.), and what I do for fun, such as sports teams or choir practice. If you need more room, go ahead and add more categories.

Go back to the first category you listed. Write the names of three people you associate with in this environment under the category heading. These people could be friends, other business people, or just those you enjoy talking with. Think of people who you know would be willing to help you. They will be your foundation for future networking.

```
                      Networking Worksheet
1. _____      5. _____
   _____         _____
   _____         _____
   _____         _____

2. _____      6. _____
   _____         _____
   _____         _____
   _____         _____

3. _____      7. _____
   _____         _____
   _____         _____
   _____         _____

4. _____      8. _____
   _____         _____
   _____         _____
   _____         _____
```

Now, go back to each of the remaining seven categories you listed above. Write the names of three people under each category. You may find it helpful to get out your address book while compiling this list. The people you'll list are the ones you find yourself calling upon when you need help or information. When you have completed your list, you should have 24 people as a part of your people resource file. This is a great place to start.

YOUR NETWORKING STRATEGY

Now it's time to take your show on the road. Let's look at some tips and techniques for making networking events a success for you.

Remember the goal setting you did on page 44 to determine what you wanted to accomplish from your networking efforts? You begin with the same idea, only this time the goal is much smaller and more specific. For example, let's say you were looking for an individual to design marketing materials for you. You are about to attend a chamber mixer and have an hour and a half to achieve this goal. Try the "3-2-1" strategy.

Networking by the Numbers

Begin by talking casually with three people who may have used the services of a marketing consultant or designer, and ask them about it. From these conversations, narrow the field to two people who actually used someone who does exactly what you need. From these two connections, maybe one will offer to introduce you directly to the designer. Set one appointment to meet the designer within a week of this event. Do you see how your three general contacts "funneled down" to one productive appointment?

This 3-2-1 strategy is very helpful if you are shy about meeting people. Goals help you to be focused and give you something specific to talk about and accomplish. (When you're looking for a resource—like the graphic designer—you generally have to talk to fewer people than when you're looking for contacts for yourself. Then you might need a 5-3-1 strategy.)

1 Useful Contact

Business Cards: The "Rule of 10"

The most common mistake I see people make is not having business cards with them at all times! It's not unusual to observe two people exchange information and watch one of them reach over to the food table and grab a paper napkin to write on. This doesn't make a very good first impression.

Apply the "Rule of 10." Take a stack of your business cards and place 10 cards in the pockets of a couple of jackets you would most likely wear

He's No Drip

Dusty Leer, of Sausalito Underwater Search, knows the value of keeping business cards handy. His business card is plastic. It is a novelty, so it gets attention, and it's also practical. People often ask him for his card when he's just out of the water, before he's had a chance to dry off. He keeps business cards in his wet suit and surprises people by having one ready to offer them.

—Rick Crandall, *1001 Ways to Market Your Services*

to networking events. Also put 10 cards in each handbag, briefcase, and organizer you carry. As a last resort, put 10 cards in the glove compartment of your car. This ensures that you never arrive anywhere without them.

Get into the habit of having cards with you wherever you are. I remember a story about Susan, in Boulder, Colorado. While on a horseback trip in Arizona, she began talking with a woman in the group. When the woman learned that Susan was a real estate agent, she asked her for a card, mentioning that she wished to move to Boulder sometime. Susan had a card in her fanny pack! The two lost touch until the woman arrived in Boulder about a year and a half later. She looked up Susan, and then bought a home from her. Shortly after, a friend followed the woman to Boulder and Susan found herself selling a second house! All from having a card available in the remotest of places.

The "Golf Pencil" Tool

Always carry something to write with. I prefer a golf pencil, because of its small size—it will fit anywhere you can put business cards. With a golf pencil, you will be less likely to get ink stains from leaky pens, or holes in your pockets from pencils that are too long when you sit down.

As you exchange business cards, use the pencil to make notes on the back of the card. You may think you will remember everything about that person when you return to the office. Trust me, you won't!

What should you write? On the back of the card write: the date and place you met, any action you promised to take such as mailing a brochure or calling with information, or something to spark your memory if you wish to write a note at a later date. On the back of your card write: a good time to reach you, a price quote or estimate if applicable, or your e-mail address. Now your card will have greater value and be kept until the information is transferred to a contact management system.

Develop a Follow-up System

What should you do with the cards and information that you've gathered while networking?

When you return to your office, set aside the cards to be entered in your contact manager and do it within three days. If any follow-up action needs to take place, do it within 24 hours, if possible, and no longer than 48 hours. This is when the meeting is fresh in your mind and theirs. Send all requested information and make a note when completed.

If I don't have any specific action to take, I often jot a handwritten note just to say that I enjoyed our meeting. This puts you in the front of your new acquaintance's mind one more time, and you can enclose a second business card. You might consider preprinted notes with your logo just for this purpose. Writing these notes is a great way to make use of the time you spend in office waiting rooms, while on hold, or waiting for an appointment to show up.

Dear Joan,

I really enjoyed chatting with you yesterday about your new product line.

Let's get together soon--

Elaine

BUILD YOUR NETWORK WITH SMALL TALK

"Small talk has a potentially huge impact on how others respond to you."
—Marjorie Brody and Barbara Pachter, *Business Etiquette*

Small talk is the tool that can help you build in-person networking relationships. Small talk is much more than just talking to people. Small talk can be a focused, goal-oriented conversation. The best small talk occurs when the ideas, information, and contacts exchanged are beneficial to both parties.

Small Talk Isn't Small Time!

Many people view small talk as mindless chatter used to fill up the "dead space" in conversations. Some view small talk as being "what you say when you really don't have anything to say."

Then there are those who appear to be natural conversationalists. They can strike up a verbal exchange with just about anybody at any time. At social and business functions, they move from group to group with little effort, accepted by everyone. And, they're having fun while making important business contacts.

These super-conversationalists weren't born with the gift-of-gab. Some were shy and introverted. Some weren't sure what to talk about. But they all learned some simple techniques that allowed them to feel comfortable in social environments. I'll explain these techniques in this section. Successful people practice these skills whenever the opportunity for small talk presents itself.

Each individual's goals are different, but personal contacts are the most valuable business and personal tool. The ideas and strategies are simple and easy to understand. You will be able to put them to use *immediately* to increase the effectiveness of your small talk. You are likely already using a few of these strategies. But others may take a bit of practice before they become "yours." Use these strategies, and you will be amazed at how quickly you will become sensational at building relationships with others!

Rules for Small Talk

Face-to-face conversations allow the participants to focus on each other. Let's say you're talking with Diane. You can find out what Diane's interests are. You can tell her about yourself and what you're looking for. Diane can ask questions of you. The information she gains about you and your business allows her to effectively relate your message to others. After one-on-one contact, prospective clients are more likely to come directly to you for products or services. They feel that they know you and people like to do business with people they know.

How Do I Make My Conversations Sound "Natural?"

1. Have conversation starters ready. In lieu of beginning with an in-depth question, sometimes you just need a conversation starter—a few words that make you feel comfortable when approaching someone you don't know. Conversation starters are opening lines that are meant to "break the ice" with someone. They are designed to get a conversation off the ground. If you see someone standing alone, go ahead and be the first one to approach and start talking. Believe me, it can feel awkward to be alone in a crowded room, and your words will be welcomed.

A few months ago, I was talking with the training director of a large corporation about conversational networking. He's an outgoing individual with a very pleasing personality. I was impressed by his ability to engage anyone in conversation, and I told him so. He chuckled at my comment and handed me an old yellow folded piece of paper from his wallet. "I've had to work at being a good conversationalist, and this has helped," he replied. I opened the paper to find a list of 10 conversation starters that he

Why Do People Talk About "the Weather?"

Sometimes small talk seems to consist of conversations about the weather, sports, current news, politics, etc. This is because these topics are safe ways to start a conversation. In our diverse culture, they're things we can all share. So don't look down on talking about the weather; use it as a springboard to "deeper" topics.

9 Ways to Open a Conversation

Here are some conversation starters you might add to your own list:

- Do you remember...?
- This is a really great place.
- Can you tell me a bit about (this organization, event, etc.)?
- Is your trip starting or ending in...(city)? (for use on an airplane).
- This is my first time here—what about you?
- I didn't realize there would be so many people here.
- I heard that you have knowledge of...may I borrow some experience?
- Have you ever thought about?
- It appears there are two of us who don't know many others here (use to approach someone who is standing alone).

carries with him all the time! So, don't feel bad if you need a little help—you're in good company.

2. Be yourself. You don't have to be "on" all the time if it's not your style. I don't expect you to be the life of the party—unless that's natural for you. Decide on what topics you are comfortable talking about at first meetings. They might be general topics like sports, TV, or current events. Or they might be your hobbies, job, or other interests. You don't have to start from scratch in every conversation. Decide on a few good lines you can use to start conversations rolling. Then you can adapt as the conversation develops. Allow your normal conversational style to come through. You make a lousy "somebody else," but you make a great *you*. Remember that!

3. Talk about them. When I first began dating, my mother gave me this advice: "When you talk to a boy, don't talk about yourself, talk about him. Ask him about his interests and he'll like you better!" Luckily, we've come a long way since then, but following the heart of that advice truly does make a good conversationalist. People always have a favorite topic, and often it's themselves! You can initially engage someone in a conversation by asking questions that allow them to talk about their business, their hobbies, or their family. Once rapport is established, it's easier for the topic to turn back to your business.

4. Ask lots of questions. Asking questions puts you in control of the conversation while featuring your conversation partner. It's an easy way to carry a conversation. And when other people do most of the talking, they remember you as a great conver-

Questions to Keep the Conversation Going

Some of my favorite questions are:
- Have you ever tried...?
- Have you been here before?
- Where are you from?
- Who do you know here?

sationalist! Ask questions, or make statements that are designed to elicit a response.

To build rapport, get people talking about topics they're comfortable with, such as themselves and their interests. A great question that only one in a hundred people asks is, "What would be a good referral for you?"

After they've talked, most people who are relationship-oriented will ask about you. Here are statements and questions that can get you what you need:

"I'm having a problem with..."

"Who do you know who...?"

"I'm looking for..."

"Have you ever had experience with...?"

"I need..."

"Would you be able to help me with...?"

When you ask questions, be sure to listen to the answers and process the information you receive. Don't spend all your time trying to think about what you're going to say next. Actively listen to others' responses. Their responses should prompt new questions from you. Then the conversation goes somewhere.

5. Find common ground with your conversational partner. What do the two of you have in

How to Be a Good Listener

Show that you are listening with nonverbal signals also. Be attentive to other people while they are speaking. Smile at them and nod your head in agreement when appropriate. Try to keep your body language "open" by not folding your arms.

Eye contact is the best way for you to show you are listening. It's rude to be constantly looking over your partner's shoulder, or around the room as if you are waiting for "someone better" to come along.

If you really feel you need to extricate yourself from this conversation, then wait for a polite opening that allows you to leave.

common that you can talk about. At many business events, people will have name tags. Maybe there is something unique about their name or business name. The name of my business, "Frankly Speaking...", is unusual and prompts questions as to how I selected it. I've been known to approach someone whose last name is "Gray" and let them know that Gray was my maiden name. Now we have something in common. Asking where someone grew up or what they like about their business also opens the door.

Is there a key to being a good "small talker"? Actually, the key is not *talking*, it's *listening!* You must learn how to be an active listener. Keep in mind that you were born with two ears and one mouth. There's an old saying that you should use them in those proportions! You never learn anything while you're talking. Being an active listener involves letting your partner know that you understand what he or she is saying. Occasionally you can paraphrase back your understanding of the message. "So, you think I should be in touch with..." is one way to do that.

Summary

Good small talk might be summarized this way:
- be comfortable with topics to open a simple conversation
- ask questions and get them talking about themselves
- find common ground
- look for ways to share valuable information
- follow-up with further networking in person and in writing

CONCLUSION

As you can see, networking and small talk can make a big difference in your success. Your job is to develop areas you're comfortable talking about. Then go out and network to help your preparation meet your opportunities!

Actively search out and use all networking opportunities as they present themselves. Try to attend at least one activity designed for networking each week. You will even balance your life better by scheduling yourself to do more activities you like. They will bring you in contact with people who share your interests.

The best advice I can give is: Don't sit in the background! Be prepared to mingle, wherever you are, even if you are uncomfortable. You will get better with practice. The more people you talk with, the more you'll help others and yourself. And the more ideas you'll have to talk about to the next person.

Good luck, and enjoy the process!

ACTION SUMMARY

"Big shots are little shots who kept shooting."
—Christopher Morley

1 Calculate how many people you need to network with to get a lead or job.

2 Make a list of people you know in different areas of your life, like church or leisure time.

3 Put business cards in your car, purse or wallet, coat pockets, etc.

4 Keep up on at least three general topics you're comfortable making small talk about.

5 Decide what specific conversation starters you're comfortable with.

6 Compile a list of questions you can ask that help you get to know others. Mentally rehearse asking them.

7 Practice specific listening skills in each conversation.

8 Have a list of things you can easily help others with.

9 Have a list of things you would like to receive.

Chapter 4

DON'T SELL—HELP PEOPLE BUY
Service Is Everyone's Job

Linda F. Fracassi

Linda F. Fracassi began her sales career in 1979 as a line telephone sales representative. She has since educated over 15,000 people on how to use the telephone to its maximum sales and service potential.

She is president of her own firm, Learning Essentials, Inc. Clients include Sony; Duracell Battery; New England Telephone; DuPont Safety; Hewlett-Packard; Providian Life Insurance; Bayer, Inc.; SKF USA; and Nobody Beats the Wiz.

Since 1988, Ms. Fracassi has been writing a regular column for the monthly newsletter *The Telephone Selling Report*, and is author of the cassette series, "How to Provide Excellent Customer Service." Ms. Fracassi released audio and video versions of the program "Service: It's a Strategy, Not a Transaction" in 1997.

Ms. Fracassi started her career as an educator at Notre Dame High School. She received her Bachelor of Arts degree from Georgian Court College.

Linda F. Fracassi, Learning Essentials, Inc., P.O. Box 5141, Toms River, NJ 08754; phone (732) 341-7356; fax (732) 341-8145; e-mail leinc@aol.com; Web site www.LearningEssentials.com.

DON'T SELL—HELP PEOPLE BUY
Service Is Everyone's Job

Linda F. Fracassi

"Render a service if you would succeed."
—Henry Miller

The best marketing you can do is to serve your existing customers in a superior way. Repeat business can account for 60 percent or more of your business. That's why everyone in any organization is involved in marketing—whether they think about it or not!

The second best way to get business is through word-of-mouth referrals. A good referral brings people to you who are presold on your benefits. You can get referrals from customers, friends, professional advisors, and even competitors. What most people forget, however, is that you receive word-of-mouth recommendations *whether you want them or not*—you just can't tell if they're good or bad!

A MIXED REFERRAL

I belong to three professional associations. Unfortunately, every time I recommend membership to prospective members, I have to include disclaimers. In a supreme case of irony, I issue the strongest disclaimer when I refer potential members to a customer service association.

"Now, Judy, I've told you this association is worth joining. You'll benefit from their educational programs and the networking. Don't get teed off when you call the association for information."

"What are you talking about? Didn't you tell me this is a service organization?"

"Yes."

"Are you telling me they don't do a stellar job of modeling the right kind of customer service? Like I'm going to be so impressed with the way they handle themselves on the telephone, I'm going to be so inspired by their level of service, that I'm going to join their association and buy their products and attend their meetings because I'll want to transfer their expertise to the hands and voices of my employees?"

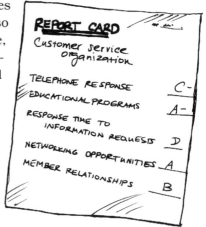

REPORT CARD
Customer Service organization

TELEPHONE RESPONSE	C-
EDUCATIONAL PROGRAMS	A-
RESPONSE TIME TO INFORMATION REQUESTS	D
NETWORKING OPPORTUNITIES	A
MEMBER RELATIONSHIPS	B

"Judy, let me put it this way. Your request for information will be treated with no urgency. Your telephone call will be treated like an interruption—that is, if you can even get a live person to talk to. Their voice mail prompting and choices are so long that if they were an ambulance service that you needed, you'd be dead before you got to the right prompt!"

"And you're sure this association is worth belonging to?"

"Yes. The networking and educational sessions are worth your time and money."

"Okay if you say so, Linda. Thanks for the warning."

Of course, they always call me back after they have spoken to the association and tell me new horror stories. I always cringe because I have not exaggerated.

Selling and Service Is a Bother?

At the annual conference of this service organization, I observed a prospective member ask the executive director why he should join. The director mentioned the newsletter and the conference as benefits. He wasn't satisfied that these two features answered the question, "What's in it for me?"

She brushed him off and walked away.

If the executive director could not summon benefits for the prospective member, is it any wonder the organization thought selling was beneath them. Maybe they believe in the *Field of Dreams* marketing method: "If you build it, they will come."

All Customer Contacts Are Important

"The thoughtless remark by a clerk. The rudeness just for a moment that infuriates the paying customer. Arrogance... indifference to a complaint...the refusal to stretch the rules just a bit to accommodate a customer with a special request.

"Thousands and thousands of dollars in future business go down the drain daily...all because simple common sense treatment of customers hasn't penetrated down the full length of the customer ladder—down to where the customer is...."

—Ray Considine and Ted Cohn, *WAYMISH: Why Are You Making It So Hard for Me to Give You My Money?*

BUT MY JOB TITLE ISN'T SALES!

Because tasks are broken up among people and titles, we can be lulled into believing that salespeople sell and are responsible for sales, customer service people provide service and are responsible for service, and marketing people come up with new and exciting ways to market our company's products and services.

Phooey!!!

You are "the company" whenever you have contact with someone outside. Let's say you're the receptionist in a dentist's office. How you greet customers can make all the difference in how they feel about their visit. After all, they may spend more time with you than the dentist. Or you're the service technician on a repair visit. When the customer asks you why it took a day to respond to their call and you say, "We're understaffed and disorganized," you've just hurt the next sale to this customer.

Moments of Truth

When he turned around Scandinavian Air, Jan Carlzon referred to every customer contact as a moment of truth. We may not think it's important, but the prospect or customer judges us from those moments. When the opportunities present themselves, it is everyone's responsibility to do the right thing. When we don't, we give our customers the motivation to start looking elsewhere for their goods and services.

I entered a very expensive, fine leather goods store to exchange a briefcase, given to me as a birthday present, for a pocketbook. The saleswoman opened the box I presented, unwrapped the tissue paper, lifted the briefcase up and out of the box, and thoroughly examined it.

She pointed out some dirt discoloration and a pen mark on the bottom. I shrugged.

She announced that she had no intention of making the exchange. She said she had no idea where the briefcase was purchased. She assured me the briefcase could not have been purchased in an authorized store.

I contacted the gift giver. She was embarrassed and incensed. She handled the exchange at

Nonprofits Market Too

Nonprofits have customers, too. They might be called donors, or volunteers, as well as beneficiaries. In fundraising and board recruitment, you are making a "sale" directly. You need publicity, you sell your ideas, and you "position" your group so the community will better understand the unique benefits you offer.

"If you want to become the greatest in your field, no matter what it may be, equip yourself to render greater service than anyone else."
— Clifton Davidson

Remember...

...the words of Benjamin Franklin (at the signing of the Declaration of Independence): "We must all hang together or we all hang separately."

...and Vidal Sassoon, "When you look good, we look good."

the store closest to her, not the store to which I had gone. The gift giver told her store of my experience. They beseeched her for the name of the saleswoman who waited on me. They wanted to have her fired. The gift giver was mollified. I was not.

The damage had already been done by this saleswoman. How much other damage had she done?

The question that begs an answer is this, regardless of the store's return policy, was it necessary for the saleswoman to imply that:

- the briefcase had been used by me or the gift giver?
- the briefcase was purchased at an unauthorized dealer, a flea market, the street corner, or out of the trunk of someone's car?

I don't think so.

If she were persuaded by the briefcase's appearance that it could not have been sold by an authorized dealer, she had other options. She could have asked me for the gift giver's name and store location, both of which I could have provided. She could have excused herself from the front counter, and called the other store to raise holy heck *with them*, instead of displaying a holier-than-thou-attitude, "We here at this store would never have sold you a briefcase in *that* condition."

If her behavior provided her with a momentary lift of superiority, look what it cost her. She upset the gift giver who was assured at the time of her purchase that the briefcase could be easily exchanged. I wasted my time with an extra trip to that store and now give the store negative word-of-mouth advertising.

HOW DO *YOU* TALK ABOUT CUSTOMERS?

My husband and I were sitting in a travel agent's office. We had our checkbook in hand. We were there to pay for a Caribbean cruise. The agent's telephone rang. She excused herself and took the call.

My attention was drawn to her conversation when I heard her say, "Unfortunately, I'm with customers now. Please call me back."

Unfortunately? Yes. You read the word correctly. Unfortunately. Hey, lady, didn't you happen to notice the checkbook in my hand? Didn't you remember that I'll be writing you a check which contains four digits?! How can that possibly be unfortunate?

We Customers Can Be "Touchy"

The only way it could be "unfortunately" is if she wanted to be unemployed. That's what happens when your lobby is empty or your telephones are silent because you have driven your customers away by your language usage!

Adding to the insult of using the word "unfortunately" in our earshot, or should I say "face shot" because we were sitting right in front of her, she then asked the customer on the phone to call *her* back. Call her back! Why would that customer call her back? Especially when they have already been told being a customer is an unfortunate situation. Why wouldn't that customer just call another travel agent? The last time I looked, there was more than one travel agency listed in the yellow pages.

Am I overreacting? I'm the customer, I can react any way I want! She could have simply said, "Since I cannot give you my full attention, may I have your name and telephone number and I will call you back within the hour [or whatever time frame is feasible]?"

"It's not the employer who pays the wages. Employers only handle the money. It is the customer who pays the wages."

—Henry Ford

I'm not trying to add more stress and pressure to your life. The objective is that the customer has a realistic expectation of your next action. You have the opportunity to meet that expectation or exceed it. That's not selling. That's helping customers buy.

This travel agent didn't do any of that. She made a poor impression on us and lost our repeat business, and she lost a potential customer.

You will increase your sales when you

- underpromise
- overdeliver
- get agreement and permission from the customer
- set clear expectations with the customer

Why Say That in Front of the Customers?

I was waiting in line at a department store. One of the saleswomen said, "I'm going to lunch, now! I've got to get out of here!"

She collected her belongings and stormed away from the counter. The saleswoman who replaced her looked a little sheepish as she took her place behind the counter. The customer in front of me turned and said, "Is that professional? Every time I come here, I swear it will be the last time. Then they have a sale and I come back."

Sounds like the language used by an addict. This customer is addicted to the store's sales. When the store has a good one, she is there. When they don't, she is not. No customer loyalty there.

I was at my bank on a holiday. While I was awaiting my turn, I heard the tellers complaining that they had to work on the holiday. They mentioned that the library was closed and griped that the bank was open.

Why did they complain in earshot of a lobby filled with bank customers? In one way, I was glad they said something. I had planned to go to the

> "The loss of focus on the customer as a human being is probably the single most important fact about the state of customer service...today."
> —Karl Albrecht,
> *The Only Thing That Matters: Bringing the Power of the Customer into the Center of Your Business*

library that afternoon so they saved me a trip. On the other hand, I'm a customer and they insulted me—and all the other waiting customers—right in front of us. Jeez, at least wait until I get in my car and drive away.

The Point Is Personal

What I find so startling about the tellers' behavior is that they can be replaced by automatic tellers. With service attitudes this cold, why won't more and more bank customers use their bank cards for all of their transactions?

Even the bank's vice president only got half the point. He wanted all of his tellers to model their behavior after one of the senior tellers, Pat. Pat knows every bank customer by name and greets them personally when they come into the bank. She usually adds something to her greeting,

"How is the new baby?"

"How was vacation?"

"How's your dad feeling since his surgery?"

And this is regardless of whether she is waiting on you or not!

She is pretty amazing to witness since the rest of the tellers are mute, unless they are speaking to each other. The VP decided he wanted everyone to address their customers by name. He instituted a procedure. There were signs posted on all the counters that read, "If I don't use your name during our transaction, ask me for a free gift."

This was his way of training his people. Something really bothers me about the VP's solution. First, he forgot in whose best interest it was to learn the customers' names: *the tellers!* Customers don't care about a gift. They care about service. To add insult to injury, he put the onus on the customer:

"If I don't use your name during our transaction, ask me for a free gift."

Now it is the customers' responsibility, not the bank tellers'. (And, I'd be willing to bet that there was a punitive system in place for those tellers who gave away too many gifts.) It was training he was doing, not educating. None of the tellers who called me by name during the gift giving, continue to use my name today. Only Pat. She *knows* her customers and does what she does out of the goodness of her heart. What she doesn't realize, is that this is really good for business.

What Do Customers Want?

A bank was trying to improve its customer service. By doing some basic research, it was determined that customers felt they were receiving good service when a teller: (1) smiled, (2) referred to the customer by name, (3) processed the transaction as quickly as possible, (4) mentioned a nonbusiness topic like the weather, and (5) thanked the customers for their business. Once you have isolated the behaviors customers desire, you need to establish goals for your employees and praise their progress toward achieving them.

—Ken Blanchard

Think Before You Speak

Sometimes we have good intentions but the language we use to express ourselves does not serve our purposes well. I was in my bank lobby one winter day. (You actually flinched when you read that didn't you. You're thinking, "Oh, no. Now what?") The lobby was filled with customers who, like me, had braved the snowy afternoon. When it was my turn to be served, I noticed the teller waiting on her computer. She mentioned how slow they were today. I looked at her and at the snow falling down outside and said, "Maybe it has something to do with the weather."

She nodded her head in agreement and said, "That's why we can't get rid of the customers."

I looked at her in amazement! Get *rid* of the customers! I thought to myself, "Well, keep this up and I'm sure you'll be successful. ATM machine, here I come!"

If I'd invited the bank teller to defend her statement, I'm sure she'd be dismayed to discover my reaction. I don't believe her intention was to insult me, but insult me she did. I believe her intention was to offer an explanation as to why transactions were taking so long on that snowy afternoon.

The Phone Counts, Too

Fie on you when you forget the words in that song by the musical group, Police: "Every move you make, every breath you take, I'll be watching you."

For those of you who use the telephone primarily for your customer communications, remember that telephone microphones are very sensitive. Customers can hear you sigh and mumble. They can't see you, but they can hear "every move you make, every breath you take."

What to Do?

When you "put on the company uniform," you represent your organization. Each time you interact with customers, you have the opportunity to welcome them or discourage them. The experiences they have with you will either continue to build upon their prior pleasant experiences, or you'll be providing them with reasons to look elsewhere.

You can make your job more secure, or you can sow the seeds for a competitor to come in and take over. Nordstrom moved from the being a west coast store to a national department store. When they went head to head with Macy's in the northeast, the exchange left Macy's in Chapter 11. And Nordstrom continues to do well against competitors that had years of experience in markets they entered.

Why Customers End the Business Relationship

48% dissatisfaction with in-person customer service

42% dissatisfaction with telephone customer service

29% dissatisfaction with automatic attendant

(respondents could name more than one reason)

Survey conducted by Nancy Friedman, The Telephone Doctor.

When Nordstrom clerks call customers and tell them that a line they like has new items in, most people appreciate the personal service. But it is also selling. Are there services or products you could be offering customers that could benefit them?

AVOID THESE WORDS

As they say, "You only get one chance to make a good first impression." Small differences in what you say can make a big difference in your customer relationships.

Here are words to avoid in your customer conversations. In most cases, customers stop listening whenever they hear these words.

- "You have to..."
- "Our policy is..."
- "That's not my department."

These are phrases a parent uses in speaking to a child, a superior to an inferior, or an uncaring bureaucrat to a powerless constituent. When we hear them, they make us feel that we are being

---

What Keeps Customers?
by Tom Peters

Attentiveness is the most powerful force in the universe.

Consider some meticulous research done by the Forum Corp. Fifteen percent of those who switched to a competitor did so because they "found a better product." Another 15% changed suppliers because they found a "cheaper product" elsewhere. Twenty percent high-tailed it because of the "lack of contact and individual attention" from the prior supplier; and 49% left because "contact form the old supplier's personnel was poor in quality." It seems fair to combine the last two categories, after which we could say 70% defected because they didn't like the human side of doing business with the previous product or service provider.

Very few companies directly look for spirit and caring in would-be employees. Then, allow (encourage! demand!) all employees to express their personalities, and, reluctantly, weed out those who fail to measure up on the attentiveness dimension. Sadly, most bosses—of 30-table restaurants and $3.5 billion department store chains—fail to put the humble issue of attentiveness at, or even near, the top of their strategic agendas.

treated like children instead of adults. They make us bristle. They certainly do not encourage us to be cooperative. They encourage us to get emotional and rebel.

"You Have To..."

Do not be misled into thinking, "Well, the customer has to do thus and such, so why can't I just say, 'You have to?'" Isn't this just playing a word game when we both know the customer has to?"

No. Providing memorable service is all about customer perceptions based on our word usage. Effective word usage goes a long way in building and maintaining customer loyalty.

In one of my customer service seminars, an attendee said, "Well, the customer *has* to give me his credit card number." I asked why. Her answer: "When customers call to register for our classes, only their credit card number will guarantee their seat." My suggestion to her was to communicate the reason to the customer in another way—a way that respects the customer. Example: "If you'll give me your credit card number, I can reserve your seat."

In situations where you want to create urgency, you can say, "If I don't have your credit card number, I won't be able to reserve your seat." This technique is called negative selling. It's when you take away the item from your customer.

I heard a customer service rep use this technique very effectively one afternoon. He received a call from a customer who was considering making reservations.

After speaking to the rep, the customer said she was going to think about it. The rep said that would be fine. In closing, he added, "I just want you to know that when you call back, the show may be sold out." She thought about it and said, "Okay, I'll book it now."

> "The more mature I get, the more I recognize the importance of listening to the customer. I won't find out what he needs if I'm doing all the talking."
> —Danielle Kennedy

USE THESE WORDS

Here are three phrases you can use effectively in place of "you have to":

"If you'll..."

"You'll want to..."

"Would you mind...?"

Your customers are more likely to listen and respond to your requests for action when they hear these phrases. These are the phrases one adult is more likely to use with another.

"Yabut"

Another word to eliminate from your customer communications is "but." Personally, I wish it could be eliminated from everyone's communications, not just customer communications. When people agree with you and then say "but," it's annoying.

I feel strongly about this for this simple, powerful reason: Whenever we hear "but," we stop listening. Period. It can be the person on the telephone, our friend, our spouse. We stop listening because we know what has preceded the "but" has now been negated. So why use it in conversation?

How do you feel when your boss tells you, you're doing a good job, but...? Doesn't "but" take away the good job? Aren't you waiting for the other shoe to drop?

I won't give you a word to use in its place. What's the point? You'd end up in the same place. Instead, eliminate the word from your vocabulary. You will find you just have two separate sentences or are now joining two phrases together with an "and" instead of the "but."

Thrill Customers

At the Ritz Carlton Hotels, each employee has a personal fund of $2,000 a year to spend on extras to delight customers. This not only gives them the means, but pushes them to look for ways to thrill customers.

CONCLUSION

Building customer relationships through great service is the best thing you can do. You'll enjoy your job more—and ensure you will be needed. After all, you're getting paid to interact with nice people.

If your intention is to help people, it will show. And it will improve the success of your organization. You can be a pleasure to do business with. When your customers ask you a question, answer repeatedly, "I can do that."

We were at the Peabody Hotel in Orlando, Florida. Upon checking in, we were told our rooms were not ready. Before I had the chance to say a single word, the man checking us in said, "Here are two coupons to enjoy a drink at our bar. When your room is ready, we will come and get you." No time to complain. No time to object. Just the time to be impressed by his initiative. That's not selling. That's helping customers buy!

ACTION SUMMARY

"Things may come to those who wait, but only those things that are left behind by those who hustle!"

—Abraham Lincoln

1 List your customers, both external and internal.

2 In what ways are you taking them for granted? In what ways could you easily show them that you care about them?

3 Are you learning customers' names and the things they care about in life?

4 Do you have any policies, such as on exchanges, that penalize the 95 percent of your customers who are honest?

5 Do you use any phrases that customers may be offended by?

6 In what ways can you overdeliver by providing more than people expect?

7 In what ways can you improve how you represent your organization to outsiders? When people ask you where you work, do you say "I work at the best _____ in town?" Why not?

Chapter 5

SERVANT SELLING

Bill Blades

Bill Blades,
CMC, CPS, is a consultant, speaker, and author. At the age of 22, he served as plant manager for a major manufacturing firm while a full-time college student. Later, while serving as vice president of sales and marketing for a food manufacturing concern, he increased sales nearly 150 percent from $13 million to $33 million in only four years. His firm was named Small Business of the Year and was always the top marketing firm in the food manufacturing area.

Mr. Blades is the author of the bestseller, *Selling: The Mother of all Enterprise*. In addition, he is featured with noted attorney F. Lee Bailey in the book *Leadership Strategists*.

One of only 51 Certified Management Consultants in the U.S. who speaks and consults with clients in the areas of sales and marketing, Mr. Blades does so with a straightforward mission statement: Our mission is to always deliver more than we promise and to serve as our clients' partners in the quest for excellence. His clients include Buick, ConAgra, GTE, and Motorola.

Bill Blades, William Blades & Associates, Ltd., 11126 East Breathless Drive, Gold Canyon, AZ 85219; phone (602) 671-3000; fax (602) 671-0926.

Chapter 5

SERVANT SELLING

Bill Blades

"Today's salesperson's greatest gift is being able to help a customer grow the business so the consultative seller's business can be grown by high-margin sales in return."

—Mack Hanan, *Consultative Selling*

Repeat business and referrals are the heart of business success. In every organization, whether big or small, whether nonprofit or for-profit, marketing must be *everyone's* responsibility. Why? Because marketing is what you do to get and keep customers. And, in order to generate repeat business and referrals, customers must receive support from both those who serve them directly, and the unseen staff whose contributions are behind the scenes.

ALL ARE CALLED, BUT FEW REALLY SERVE

In the United States, many people are uncomfortable with the word "servant." Many think that by serving others, they are diminished. But nothing could be further from the truth. You grow the most as a human being by helping others.

The term "servant leadership" was coined by Robert Greenleaf. The concept of servant leadership is that leaders serve their employees, not command them. It's the idea of the organizational pyramid being turned upside down.

In this upside-down structure, the customer is on top, supported by the front lines, with the executives underneath to support the rest. Servant leadership also has a Biblical meaning—that we are on this earth to serve others and, by doing so, we achieve happiness. (Unfortunately, most executives don't exemplify a true service mentality. So naturally, employees and salespeople don't either.)

I use the term "servant sales" in the same sense of true service. You act as a consultant to help people better understand their needs. With servant selling, you sell and advance your own interests only by helping others achieve their goals.

Consultative Selling™, Relationship Marketing, Etc.

Many terms relate to servant selling. Perhaps the most general is "relationship marketing." Several books have been written using this title. These books reinforce the general idea that building relationships with prospects and customers will help you be successful.

Perhaps the most developed, related term is Consultative Selling™ (created and trademarked by Mack Hanan in 1970). Hanan uses it to describe a process in which you improve your customers' returns on investments by bringing them solutions to their problems, and then partnering with them to implement the solutions. However, many others use this term in a more generic sense of building relationships with customers and acting like a consultant.

"You can get anything you want in life if you first help other people get what they want."
—Zig Ziglar

"The mark of good salespeople is that customers don't regard them as salespeople at all, but as trusted and indispensable advisors, auxiliary employees who, fortunately, are on someone else's payroll."
—Harvey Mackay

FIVE STEPS FOR SERVANT SELLING

I've broken servant selling down into five key areas to help you organize your own approaches: *building relationships, analyzing needs, knowing your customers' industries, generating creative ideas,* and *helping your customers succeed.* If you're in sales, you should become proficient in all five areas. If your job does not directly involve sales, you will probably contribute in fewer areas.

Step 1: Building Relationships

Everyone can contribute to building relationships with prospects and customers. In fact, customers are often more impressed when the person answering the phone remembers them than when a salesperson makes a bigger effort to be friendly. Everyone wants to be treated as special. Every customer contact is an opportunity to do that. Yet most organizations waste their chances.

Relationships can be built around business or personal issues. Mark McCormack, author of *What They Don't Teach You at Harvard Business School,* says that other things being equal, people do business with people they like. And other things not being equal, they *still* do business with people they like! Do things that will help your prospects and customers like you.

Individual Differences. People are like thumbprints—no two are alike. To build relationships, you have to treat people differently! Yet many salespeople make every sales call the same.

One method for classifying general types of behavior is the DISC. I am the classic High D

Bottom-Up Marketing

One smart industrial-and-commercial building contractor gave all his employees business cards. A secretary from his firm was attending the symphony with her husband when she met a man who talked about needing another office building. She gave him her card, he called, and the contractor ended up getting the job. When employees have their own cards, they feel a greater bond with the company and you capture more opportunities.

JOE'S Construction

Jane Ferrari
office manager

(123)555 1000

(Dominance behavior) and High I (Influencing behavior) guy. On the S and C dimensions (Steadiness and Conscientious behaviors), I'm very low.

High D/High I people love to talk. A salesperson cannot come in and call on me, yapping away. Salespeople better be doing two things: They better give me an idea that can potentially help me. And they better get straight to the point.

An understanding of the four DISC behavior styles will allow you to tailor your approach to the individual. With the Steady-type person, you'll probably want to sit over a cup of coffee and just shoot the breeze for about five minutes before you start. With people like me, you start the first minute you get there. When you're doing servant selling, you've got to be aware and use different styles for different people, even though your goal is still the same.

Step 2: Analyzing Needs

Most salespeople have their talk-listen ratio out of whack. An old saying in sales is that you have two ears and one mouth and you should use them in that proportion. That saying doesn't go far enough. Great needs analysis selling is:

> ### One-to-One Marketing
>
> "We've reached the point where technology allows us to do mass customization, one-to-one. Your target should be one person, and you should be dealing with them differently than each other person in the target market."
>
> —Don Peppers and Martha Rogers, *The One to One Future: Building Relationships One Customer at a Time*

(1) 90 percent asking targeted questions,

(2) listening intently to every single word, and

(3) taking great notes.

Listen More Than You Speak. Needs analysis selling is only 10 percent talking. That's another reason why everyone in a company can help sell. They can all gather information from prospects and clients as respectful listeners.

When you're talking, people only have a three-sentence attention span on average. If they have an active mind, after three or four sentences, you'd better be asking a question. Unfortunately, when a lot of a salespeople are supposedly listening to a client they're thinking, "I'll be glad when the client shuts up, so I can say something important."

Here's an example of a "good" conversation from the client's point of view. The client says to me, "Bill, we are taking our group to Hawaii."

I've only a one-word question: "Hawaii?"

"Yeah, we're going over to Maui. It's an incentive trip."

"Incentive?"

"Yeah, every year we take the top ten..." and it goes on and on and on.

Often, I only respond with a one-word question. (See Chapter 7 for more incentives.)

Needs Analysis. When I do needs analysis, I will sometimes ask questions that have nothing to do with my business. A salesperson who might be selling computers might ask, "Mr. Jones, let me ask this question so that I can learn how to help you better. Could I get a copy of your mission statement?" Or the question might be, "In your business plan, or sales and marketing plan, what's the number one thing that you are going to be working on this year?" These are good business-consulting questions.

Use Standard Forms. I use two needs analysis forms in my business. One is for speaking and the other one is for long-term consulting projects. In my absence from the office, everyone is equipped and well trained to ask the questions.

When it comes time for a long-term consulting project, I

"Problem questions probe for problems, difficulties, or dissatisfactions. Each invites the customer to state implied needs."

—Neil Rackham, SPIN Selling

get paid to go
in for three
days just to
ask questions.
And it takes us
a minimum of
two days to go
all the way
through them.
Two or three
years ago, a
c o m p a n y
president in
O k l a h o m a

> ## Needs Analysis for Speaking
> ### (abbreviated)
>
> Contact information:_____
>
> What do you do? _____
>
> Who do you sell to? _____
>
> Logistics of date, etc. _____
>
> What are your challenges? _____
>
> What did you like or dislike about
> your last speaker?_____

brought me in for a couple of days just off of my reputation. We were
in the board room with his VPs and he said, "You haven't convinced
me yet."

I said, "Sir, I've not even tried. I'm just here to find out what
needs fixing. You called me in. I'm not trying to sell anything because
in the medical field, prescription without diagnosis would be
malpractice. Every consulting project that I do is different. It's not
a canned program coming off the shelf. I need to finish asking all
these questions, then we will go back and prioritize every single
thing that needs improving. Then I will know what you want me to
do first."

He said, "I like it. Will you teach our salespeople how to do this?"

I said, "Sir, I will. I can't tell you when. It depends on your
priority list."

* * *

The Five Areas Are Integrated. I'm presenting five separate
aspects of servant selling. But, of course, in real life you don't have
to work on each one separately. For instance, listening better helps
you build relationships as well as understand prospects' needs. And
creativity can be applied to each area as the sidebar on the next page
about reading shows.

Step 3: Knowing Your Customer's Industry

Broad knowledge from many areas can be useful. But when
most people have a problem, they want an expert in that area. They

How Reading Helped Me

It pays to read widely—"industry knowledge" isn't always technical.

When I board a plane, I drop my things in my seat and go immediately to the magazine bin. I want to be the first person there.

A while ago, an association was considering hiring me to speak at an upcoming meeting in Phoenix. One of the travel magazines I saw on a plane rated four new and best restaurants in Phoenix. I cut it out and mailed it to the client with a note, "You might want to include this in your registration packet for your attendees." I got the job.

At the meeting, the executive director said, "Let me show you something." He pulled the article I'd sent him out of a registration packet—he'd put it in all the packets. And he said, "A lot of our people last night on their own went to some of these places. They appreciated that I put this article in there. Bill, we were looking at three different speakers. I was kind of leaning your way, but your sending me that fresh article showed you were thinking about me. I really appreciated that."

It wasn't that big of a deal. But it's what servant selling does. You look for things for others even when you're not hired. And when you help people in areas where you're not selling, it builds you up as a true servant seller.

don't want to have to educate you on their time! That's why focused, niche marketing is so powerful.

Educate yourself about both what your company sells and about your customers' industries. I ask people, "Would you want to buy from a salesperson who doesn't read?" You can come up with good ideas to solve their problems through what you read and who you know.

People who are serious about their businesses know more than their competitors. They usually read more than anybody else. They don't read between the hours of 8 a.m. and 5 p.m, but pay the price at night and on weekends.

Work harder for yourself than you do for your boss. Read, read, read so that you can find things that will be of interest to a client. Mark Twain said, "The man who does not read has no advantage over the man who cannot." In other words, the books and the magazines you don't read may hurt you.

Step 4: Be Creative

One way to combine other steps in this process of servant selling is through fresh, creative approaches. For instance, here's an example of how I started with needs analysis to help a client succeed.

A client of mine, DW Distribution, was planning their exhibit at a big trade show. I asked them questions like, "Tell me exactly what you're going to exhibit at this trade show?"

"Well, our line of doors, windows, and moldings."

"Tell me what your competitors are going to exhibit?"

"I get it. Doors, windows, and moldings."

Choose a Unique Position. In order to position them differently from competitors who sold the same things, we came up with one word: Lagniappe.

That means "a little something extra" in Cajun talk. We set up a custom booth, different from prior years. At each of the four corners of the booth, there were triangular-shaped beams. We carved the word "lagniappe" on each of the three sides of each beam. People would come into the booth and ask, "What is lagniappe?" We couldn't wait for that question from each visitor.

We also sent a letter ahead of time to targeted clients and potential clients that offered my free consulting at the show. It told about my background and invited people to call and make appointments and bring their best questions. After their meetings with me, they were each given a classy gift.

We fired off "lagniappe" postcards that day so that the postcards would beat them back home. All the postcards were from DW's president: "We want to thank you for coming by. I would consider it a favor if you would

> # LAGNIAPPE
>
> We want to thank you for coming by. I would consider it a favor if you would tell me any time we can improve our services.

tell me any time we can improve our services."

Millions of dollars came to their bottom line because of that one event. I did nothing for two days but meet one-on-one with their customers and listen to their challenges. I was there to help them. Real value.

In my meetings with DW's customers and prospects, I was also able to collect lots of interesting information for the company about customer needs and attitudes. (For more on creativity in sales, also see my chapter in *Break-Out Creativity*.)

> "You are no longer a vendor, out to sell a customer a product; you are a consultant, out to help your client's business grow."
> —Mack Hanan,
> *Consultative Selling* (5th Ed.)

Step 5: Helping Your Customers Succeed

The first four steps of servant selling are all designed to help you provide value to your customers. By building relationships, you win their trust to take the relationship further. You analyze their needs and apply your knowledge of their industry and your creativity to come up with solutions for them. Then your solutions help them succeed, which builds the long-term business which is profitable for you.

Provide Objective Information. You can see that even if your job is not sales and marketing, you can be contributing to helping your customers succeed. One of the best ways to do this— offering valued-added information—builds your credibility tremendously because it doesn't involve selling what you do. Even someone very shy about the idea of selling should be comfortable with this approach.

Santa Claus Selling

If you don't have something appropriate, send people to another source. Remember Kris Kringle in *Miracle on 34th Street*? People became more loyal Macy's customers when he sent them to other stores. You build great credibility when you point out things you can't do... Good referrals to other sources show them that you really have their best interests at heart.

—Rick Crandall, *Marketing Your Services: For People Who Hate to Sell*

Here's an example from many years ago, going back to the oil embargo: I kept hearing from many clients how much money it was costing to operate their trucks. I lived in Atlanta. I called the Georgia Department of Transportation and the Georgia Trucking Association and asked, "Is there anything new that you can send to me that I might send to my clients regarding saving money on fuel." I got quite a packet of information and distributed copies to my clients.

It didn't matter if the ideas were great or not so great, my clients were "blown away." Today, you could gather this kind of information online and distribute it.

Boost Your Customers' Profits. What can you give your clients that will help them? Here's a creative idea. I often speak to my clients' customers. I will do a "CEO conference." My clients invite CEOs both from firms that buy a lot from them and from firms that are buying nothing. We strategically seat the CEOs around the breakfast tables so each table has a mixture of CEOs who can give testimonials about different aspects of the client's services. I tell the client: "Do not pass out literature. Say nothing about your company. I will brag about you one time when I'm talking about value added."

From *Key Account Selling* by Mack Hanan

After I finish my talk, the client visits each table and says, "Folks, we want to thank you for coming. We hope this was everything that we said it would be and I hope you'll stay and chat. Thank you very much." It's totally soft sell. The guests are thinking, "Wait a minute. Where's the hook?" People see that we're investing time and money to bring value to them and start viewing us as their partner.

CONCLUSION: HOLD PEOPLE ACCOUNTABLE *AND* REWARD THEM

In my sales training, I tell people that sales training by itself does not work.

You've got to do a lot of follow-up. You've got to hold people accountable for X number of new skills. You've got to monitor like crazy. That way, the investment comes back; otherwise, most people will keep acting like they did last week.

When we educate sales-people individually, we give them new assignments based on their own personality profiles by profession. We might require them to learn 12 new skills a quarter. Then they're professionals who are investing in themselves and they're better able to help clients.

If you're not in sales but have contact with customers, how you act can make all the difference in the customers' relationships with your organization.

In the glory days of IBM, receptionists and other "non-salespeople" got commissions on sales by their units. The company recognized that their behavior contributed to revenues by building customer relationships. Everyone won.

Moments of Truth

A moment of truth is when a customer forms an opinion about you or your company based on any interaction. Moments of truth can arise from seemingly small and inconsequential actions. Jan Carlzon, author of *Moments of Truth*, points out that the simple act of an airline passenger pulling down his or her tray can be a moment of truth. If a passenger sees a coffee stain that should have been cleaned up and was not, what conclusions could be drawn from this? Perhaps that if the airline cannot maintain its trays, it is sloppy at all maintenance and probably does not maintain its engines!

Work hard on developing yourself. Go the extra mile for clients by delivering unheard of value. And never stop. It's called Lagniappe.

Even if your organization isn't smart enough to reward you for contributing to customer satisfaction, you can grow as a person—and increase your value to the company—by doing so. And when you raise your value and give to others, it tends to come back to you. That's more of the beauty of servant selling.

ACTION SUMMARY

"He who has begun is half done. Dare to be wise; begin!"

—Horace

1 Make a new commitment to helping others before you expect them to help you.

2 In order to build relationships with people, you have to know things about them. Find out about your customers' and prospects' families, hobbies, and interests.

3 Study individual differences. Classify the people you come in regular contact with and see if it helps you relate to them.

4 Practice needs analysis questions.

5 Develop a needs analysis form with your best questions.

6 Be a better listener by repeating back key parts of what others say and checking your understanding.

7 Invest in yourself. Go to the library and find more magazines that would give you ideas for your clients. Then subscribe to some. (Many trade magazines are free.)

8 What can you do to creatively show people why they should work with you?

9 Write a list of ways you can help your clients and prospects so they'll be glad to talk with you.

10 Ask good customers about how you could help them with their customers.

Chapter 6

GET 100% OF THE BUSINESS FROM 100% OF YOUR CUSTOMERS

Ed Peters

Ed Peters
is an entrepreneur, author, educator, and speaker on relationship marketing and customer satisfaction. Through his Relationship Marketing Institute, he designs programs for getting and keeping customers, gives keynote speeches and seminars on "Getting 100% of the Business from 100% of Your Customers," and manages a marketing and customer satisfaction resource Web site (www.relmarketing.com).

Mr. Peters has an extensive background in marketing, including executive positions with one of the world's largest travel organizations. He has served on the national advisory boards of three hotel chains and his customer communication programs were judged best in the nation by his peers.

He has developed a headquarters for an international joint venture in The Hague and London, and was recently selected by the Indus Foundation to conduct seminars for business executives throughout India.

In addition to the Relationship Marketing Institute, Mr. Peters is an owner of a new database marketing company, a member of the prestigious National Speaker's Association, and has just completed his term as president of the Lake Forest, Illinois Chamber of Commerce.

Ed Peters, Relationship Marketing Systems, 1025 W. Everett Rd., Lake Forest, IL 60045; phone (847) 234-1995; fax (847) 234-3304; e-mail epeters@relmarketing.com.

Chapter 6

GET 100% OF THE BUSINESS FROM 100% OF YOUR CUSTOMERS

Ed Peters

"Nurture your relationships with each customer ...selling more to fewer is more efficient...and more profitable."

—Don Peppers and Martha Rogers,
The One to One Future, Building Relationships One Customer at a Time

Are you getting 100 percent of the business from your customers? Do you even know?

If you are like most business people today, you are getting only a small share of the potential business from most of your customers. Why?

Mark Twain once said, "If you always do what you always did, you'll always get what you always got." His words are brilliantly appropriate for most of us in marketing. Traditional marketing strategies seek to reach the greatest number of prospects at the lowest possible cost. These strategies actually keep us from getting 100 percent of the business from 100 percent of our customers!

WHAT 100 PERCENT IS WORTH

Now, before you say it's almost impossible to get 100 percent of the business from 100 percent of your customers, take a moment to determine what getting 100 percent of the business from 100 percent of your customers is worth. Fill in the blanks in the box on page 91. It's okay to write in the book...go ahead, I'll wait.

Are you as amazed as most people are at the staggering sum represented by 100 percent of the business from 100 percent of your customers? While getting 100 percent of the business from 100 percent of your customers is a challenging feat, isn't it now clear that the effort is worth it?

GREAT
SERVICE

⊹

MORE NEEDS
MET

⇩

100% of
BUSINESS

RELATIONSHIP MARKETING

Getting 100 percent of the business from 100 percent of your customers is achievable only through "relationship marketing." You need to understand the wants and needs of each customer and meet those needs by personalized one-to-one target marketing and unprecedented customer service.

Getting 100 percent of the business from 100 percent of your customers is accomplished through relationship marketing by:

- keeping all your existing customers through great customer service
- constantly expanding the business you get from your existing customers by meeting more of their needs
- continually developing your relation-ships with new prospects until they become customers for life and you have a wildly successful business

If you think getting 100 percent of all your customers' business is hard, what about closing

100 percent of your prospects? That's what Harvey Mackay says he does. In addition to authoring bestselling books (*Swim with the Sharks...*), his company sells envelopes. Because he never gives up on a legitimate prospect, he figures that eventually, if he keeps in touch, he'll get their business.

> "Consumers are statistics. Customers are people."
> —Neiman-Marcus

KNOW YOUR CUSTOMERS

Often I like to start my relationship marketing speeches and seminars by asking the audience to list their top ten customers, the amount of money each customer spent in the past year, and the date of the last time they saw those customers. Fewer than 10 percent of the people in my audiences know who their top ten customers are! Even fewer know how much business they've done with them over the past year. Hardly any of them can say when they've seen them last.

And that's just the top ten! If you want to get 100 percent of the business from 100 percent of your customers, you should know who all your customers are...for starters!

Lifetime Value of 100 Percent of the Business from 100 Percent of Your Customers

Fill in the chart below and you'll quickly see how important it is to keep every customer for life!

(1) Number of years expect to keep customer   _____

(2) Amount average customer spends/year   _____

(3) Multiply (1) × (2)   _____

(4) Number of current customers   _____

(5) Multiply (3) × (4) for the
Lifetime Value of 100 Percent of the Business from 100 Percent of Your Customers   _____

If you know who your customers are, you can sell them more. Granted, you have to know something about the customers. But if you do, you can target your marketing and, in the process, utilize your scarce resources in a manner which produces significant, measurable, and profitable results.

Target marketing used to mean customizing your messages for types of customers. Today with new technologies, you can build relationships—and target your messages—to each customer and prospect individually.

You can't make a connection with someone if you have nothing to talk about. In order to build individual relationships with customers, you need to know a lot about them. Harvey Mackay developed the "Mackay 66" —66 items of information his salespeople are to learn about each prospect, from their ages to their hobbies and their families' names and interests.

You may want to know 66 things or 26 or 106. But the last question on Mackay's list is whether *your competitors* know more of the answers than you do. You'll want the answer to that!

> "To establish a foundation for a relationship based on shared interests, [you need to] find out the information that will help you make a good impression."
> —Harvey Mackay, *Dig Your Well Before You're Thirsty*

THE WINNER'S CIRCLE: BUILD A DATABASE

To build relationships, you need to know people and keep track of the information. The ability to communicate with customers in a targeted way is possible only if you have an effective record keeping system. When this involves many records, it's called a customer database. In terms of delivering a specific message to a specific audience, traditional advertising media falls short. (It's usually more expensive, too!)

Can you imagine that one of the world's premier thoroughbred racetracks didn't own a customer list until a couple of years ago?!

This track, one of the most expensive ever built, depended almost entirely on traditional media advertising to entice people to visit. Hundreds of thousands of people visited each season and yet no names, addresses, or betting histories were ever recorded.

When we went to work with them, we used three methods to help the racetrack build a qualified, usable database in just three weeks!

First, we combed through nearly 100,000 names and addresses which had been collected through various "door prize" promotions the previous years. Second, we ran an additional "sign up" promotion at the track one weekend. Third, we ran an ad in the newspaper asking fans to mail or fax their names and addresses in return for a chance to win $10,000.

Seven thousand people responded. Not only did we obtain names and addresses, but also their age, numbers of days they expected to visit the track that year, and their opinions on an issue before the state racing board.

Using the Database

We took 50,000 of the most desirable names and mailed a promotion inviting them to visit the track on a particular Sunday. Inside the envelope was a betting slip we guaranteed would be worth at least $2 upon redemption. One ticket was worth $10,000. From the 50,000 invitations, 17,000 fans showed up, contributing to one of the largest gates in track history.

Technology Allows One-on-One Marketing

"Theoretically, the power of computers and databases allows products and services to be completely customized. American Express prints 1,349 versions of its newsletter for corporate card customers, with customized editorials and offers, depending on spending patterns.

"Similarly, skiers at Northstar at Tahoe are wearing wristbands, earning points towards equipment purchases. The resort uses the wristbands to track the places where customers spend the day so the resort can better tailor packages and promotions."

—*Direct* magazine

Given that admission to the track ranged from $2–$4, all the money given away from the betting slips was recovered, plus the track made additional revenue from programs, food, souvenirs, and—of course—pari-mutuel wagering.

What made the promotion successful? It was relationship marketing and that the promotion was directed to past customers.

The new database and the betting slip promotion was only part of the marketing miracle taking place at the track. We also helped the track develop a "preferred customer" program, where every visit counted toward unique prizes, such as watching a race from the announcer's booth or having your picture taken with your favorite jockey. It's no coincidence that the person who carries a "preferred customer" card is 50 percent more likely to visit the track than the fan who does not.

You can do a lot over time when you apply relationship marketing thinking and seek to get "100 percent of the business from 100 percent of your customers." Today, following the lead of the casinos, the track electronically records every wager and pays special attention to its "best" customers.

> "You run a business to satisfy the consumer. That isn't marketing. That goes way beyond marketing."
> —Peter Drucker

THE GOOD LIFE

Billy's Good Life Cafe is a new, upscale restaurant in suburban Chicago. Location, menu, food quality, atmosphere, and service combined to make the Good Life Cafe a financial success from day one.

What started more slowly was the Good Life Cafe home delivery business, dubbed "from our kitchen to your table." Customers weren't used to having food delivered from a "white tablecloth" restaurant—certainly not delivered fresh and hot. Yet the Good Life Cafe was perfectly positioned to

Measuring Customer Satisfaction

There are lots of ways to measure customer satisfaction. You can set up a customer focus group, conduct customer interviews, make customer feedback forms available, etc. You can devise your own questionnaire or use one already on the market.

Design your questions around four basic categories:

• What are we doing well and how does it compare to our competitors? (This shows you what your customers value.)
• What should we continue doing?
• What should we start doing?
• What should we stop doing?

Let your customers tell you where you should be headed. And don't limit yourself to your current customers. Occasionally, survey people who aren't your customers. Find out why you don't have their business.

The information you collect will tell you how and where you need to improve. And remember to share the information you gather with all of your employees. They won't be able to provide service from the customer's point of view if they don't know what that point of view is.

—Ken Blanchard, Blanchard Training & Development

cash in on the delivery opportunity because it was located in the heart of an area with high income, working spouses, and customers with a desire for time-saving meal preparation and a penchant for "the good life."

Sell More to Current Customers

When we took on the Good Life Cafe as a client, it seemed to us that the best home delivery prospect was the satisfied restaurant customer. After enjoying a marvelous meal in the restaurant, who's easier to convince about the benefits of having the same menu offerings delivered at home?

We distributed a "join our mailing list" card in the restaurant. To those who responded, we mailed a personal thank you note within 48 hours from Billy, the owner, and a full-size, nicely printed delivery menu.

Customer Satisfaction

We also included a brief customer satisfaction survey, the results of which we are able to track by date, lunch vs. dinner, and by server. With an ongoing response rate of nearly 23 percent, we can better understand what we're doing right and wrong, what we can do to improve the business, and even determine which wait staff provide the best service. But the real value of this effort at the Good Life Cafe is the extensive customer database we've helped develop.

The New Database

In the spring of 1997, we put that database to good use. It seemed that when the Chicago Bulls were in the playoffs (which was every year!), restaurant business in Chicago fell off drastically. Restaurant patrons, accustomed to eating out on weekends and even during the week, suddenly went to the games or stayed home to watch them. At least two well-known restaurants closed their doors permanently or filed for bankruptcy because of the Bull's success.

The Good Life Cafe took the "bulls by the horns" and decided it would increase, not decrease, its business during the playoffs. We told the customers, "...if you must stay home, consider the Good Life Cafe's home delivery" and that part of the business increased.

In addition, Billy installed small televisions throughout the restaurant so his patrons could still eat out and not miss the exciting action. Using the database we had been cultivating, we mailed a postcard to customers inviting them to watch the games and enjoy complimentary appetizers with dinner. While most Chicago restaurants experienced their annual business drop, the Good Life Cafe saw its business grow.

CUSTOMER SATISFACTION PLUS

You can't get 100 percent of the business from 100 percent of your customers unless you satisfy 100 percent of your customers 100 percent of the time—before, during, and after the sale.

And not just with good service. Good service isn't good enough. It has to be great. I call it

"Customer satisfaction does NOT lead to repeat business! There must be an emotional bond—almost a love vs. hate that predicts repeat business!"
—Robert Peterson, University of Texas

"unprecedented" service because, unless it exceeds a customer's expectations, it probably won't be noticed and won't help you get all the business you can from all your customers.

IMPROVING THE DATABASE

One of the Midwest's largest men's clothing stores had a mailing list of over 60,000 customers. The problem was, the list contained only names and addresses...no vital customer profile information such as sizes, style preferences, or attitudes about the store.

We sent a personalized letter to those 60,000 customers asking them to return a short survey with questions such as "Why do you shop here?", "How much of your business are we currently getting?", and "What is your overall satisfaction with the shopping experience?" When we processed the response, we were shocked at the result. We found that the reasons 90 percent of the customers shopped at other men's stores were the exact same reasons 10 percent of the customers shopped only at our client's stores.

Price and selection were both the heroes and the culprits. Our client charged the same prices as other stores and the product selection was the same, too. Yet, customers experienced each differently.

Without good information, our client might have rushed to lower prices or increase inventory when what he really had was a perception issue. We created a newsletter to better communicate the origin of the prices and to communicate the vast selection our client offered.

One of the relationship marketing strategies we implemented was a thank you note to every customer—about 500 a week! The letter of appreciation also asked the customer to return a brief satisfaction survey. Response to the survey was a staggering 21 percent!

A Subtle Difference

Ten thousand surveys later, we had an extraordinary problem *and* opportunity to deal with. As you can see from the graphs, customer satisfaction has a big impact on both the amount customers spend, and how many times customers visit the stores. Customers who had an "excellent" shopping experience (48 percent of them) visited the stores an average of 3.9 times a year and spent an average of $465 per visit. Customers who merely had a "good" experience (49 percent of them) visited 3.5 times a year and spent $397 per visit. The difference between a "great" experience and a "good" experience (half a visit per year and $68 per visit) was about $3.2 million a year in lost sales!

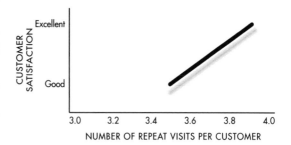

We immediately moved to improve the shopping experience: better signage, increased product training, and most of all, better interpersonal relations between the salespeople and the customers. Exchanging sales commissions for "satisfaction" commissions, the salespeople were rewarded financially every time a satisfaction survey was returned with a rating of "excellent" and the salesperson's name.

While our client's competitors spent many resources looking for new customers, we focused on moving customers from a good experience to a great experience. In eighteen months, customers who had a great experience increased from 48 percent to 67 percent, and our client realized nearly $1.2 million in additional sales at a marketing cost of less than 10 percent of that figure!

There should no surprise that satisfied customers will visit you more often and spend more money with each visit. Today, a customer who merely has a "good" experience is a customer at risk. They'll keep shopping around until they find that elusive "great" experience. And when they find it, they'll never leave because they're not willing to take a chance that the new experience won't be as great.

> "A five percentage point increase in customer retention in a typical company will increase profits by more than 25 percent, and growth by more than 100 percent!"
> —Frederick F. Reichheld, *The Loyalty Effect*

LOST OPPORTUNITIES

Want further proof that focusing on total customer satisfaction increases profits?

We had an unusual experience with one of our clients, a well-known, upscale hotel in downtown Chicago. Hotel management claimed that they were already getting nearly 100 percent of the business from 100 percent of their "best" customers—defined as customers who stayed at the hotel at least ten times a year.

What they didn't know, and painfully discovered, was that 79 percent of the business of their best customers was leaking to competitors. Sure, they were staying at our client's hotel ten nights a year, but somewhere else 20, 30, 40 or more times!

What hurt worse than the nearly $1 million in lost sales were the reasons behind the loss. Most of the customers who stayed at other hotels did so because of perceptual problems with our client's hotel.

For example, 15 percent stayed elsewhere because they didn't like taking a cab to Chicago's Loop and, yet, the hotel had a fleet of complimentary limos most "best" customers had never heard of. Another 15 percent stayed somewhere else because they were dissatisfied with the hotel's health club, yet were unaware that the hotel had recently renovated the facility.

The hotel needed a budget to communicate to its best customers. Through our survey, we knew who these "stray" customers were and why they went "astray." We could respond to them (and we did personally) about their misperceptions. But what about the thousands of customers not defined as "best" and whom we knew nothing about?

What keeps you from getting 100 percent of the business from 100 percent of your customers? It is mediocre, antiquated, unmeasurable marketing strategies and poor customer satisfaction policies.

DRIVING HOME THE POINT

Inevitably, poor marketing execution and feeble customer service can cost you money...big money.

A couple of years ago, I planned a two-week driving trip through the Southeast. Knowing that my evening stops would be unscheduled, I called Days Inn to obtain a motel directory. This way, I'd drive until I got tired and check the directory for the nearest motel. I called three weeks before my trip, but was told by the Days Inn representative that the directory would take 4–6 weeks to arrive. I told her again that I needed the directory within three weeks, but she only reiterated company policy.

Defeated, I called Motel 6 where I was assured I'd get their directory

> "As true differentiation is harder to come by and even tougher to sustain, [customer] perceptions will play a greater role in setting products and services apart from one another. That's why it's so crucial for you to [use research to] understand precisely what your business really stands for in the eyes of your target audience."
> —Jay Conrad Levinson, *Guerrilla Marketing*

"Complaints offer companies the opportunity to demonstrate their appreciation of, and interest in, the customer which can turn a disgruntled client into a satisfied, loyal, and vocal advocate."

—Janell Barlow and
Claus Møller,
A Complaint Is a Gift

immediately. The book arrived in four days—I took my trip, and spent over $350 at 10 Motel 6s.

A week after my trip, the Days Inn directory arrived! Being a savvy marketing professional, I wrote a letter to Days Inn's president, explaining my difficulty in doing business with his company. I also enclosed copies of my Motel 6 receipts so he could see the business lost because of company policy. A short time later, I received a letter from a vice president who apologized for my problem but offered no explanation or remedy. She also included a 10 percent discount coupon for my next Days Inn stay—good only for 30 days.

Do you think Days Inn missed the point?

A Big $5 Mistake

Missing sales opportunities because of a silly company policy is actually quite common. I recently called a specialty paper company, Paper Direct, to obtain a paper sample for a client for whom we were designing a brochure. I estimated the paper would cost over $700. The Paper Direct agent explained that the paper sample I needed cost $5. I replied that no other paper company had ever charged me for a sample and I wasn't about to pay for one now.

At my request, the agent connected me to a supervisor who reiterated company policy. I hung up, called a competitor, received a free sample, and eventually ordered $724 worth of paper. I wrote a letter to Paper Direct's president describing how difficult it was to do business with his company. I also enclosed a copy of his competitor's invoice. Amazingly, I got no response.

SO WHO'S DOING IT RIGHT?

I'm often asked for extraordinary examples of companies that exceed their customers' expectations. We all know about legendary service at Nordstrom's, innovative service at Stew Leonard's Dairy Store, and personal service at Southwest Airlines. But I like to talk about a little store in Dayton, Ohio, where I grew up.

It was a toy store, called Jandy's. At Jandy's, kids were the customers, not the parents. When you walked into Jandy's, the owner (Mr. Jandy we called him), was right there to say "hi." He'd take you by the hand and show you all the new toys. Unlike today's toy stores, he encouraged you to play with the toys, right in the aisles. And, the best toys at Jandy's were not on the top shelf, out of reach of clumsy kids, but on the bottom ones where we could get to them.

I learned later that my buddies and I were Mr. Jandy's focus group, and he observed us with a keen eye for which toys we liked best, how long we'd play with them, which ones broke easily, and which ones were unsafe.

Mr. Jandy got to know my dad very well (not just because he had five kids, but also because he bought thousands of toys every year for a company Christmas party). He'd send toys home with my dad for my brothers and sisters to try out, extending his research. He even hired dad to work part-time at Christmas utilizing my dad's unique ability to know what toys kids of all ages had their hearts set on. He'd pay my dad with toys and we had some magnificent mornings under the tree.

Whenever we visited Jandy's, Mr. Jandy would give us something free. It was always something

"We speak of educating our children. Do we know that our children also educate us?"

—Mrs. Sigourney

small and inexpensive, but the idea of something free to a ten year old caused many a detour on a bike ride home from school.

Jandy's Toy Store was legendary. Everybody in my neighborhood bought all their toys from Jandy's. Mr. Jandy knew something about innovative marketing and unprecedented customer service. He knew something about lifetime value and I guarantee you he knew who his top ten— make that top 500 customers—were. He knew who his customers were and he knew what they wanted. And I'm sure that Mr. Jandy got 100 percent of the business from 100 percent of his customers!

ACTION SUMMARY

"If you really want to do something, you'll find a way; if you don't, you'll find an excuse."

—*Forbes* magazine

You too can build lifetime relationships with customers and become legendary for unprecedented service that exceeds expectations. Your first step is to establish these as overall goals. Then decide on the specific steps you'll take to implement great service and relationships. In addition to those you've already thought of, here are a few action steps to consider.

1 You can't have relationships without knowing things about people. Decide what you want to know about your top 20 customers and start building client records.

2 Decide what information is practical to collect about all of your customers and write down the first steps you need to take to put that plan into effect. Consider a mail survey, a special prize drawing, or just calling people.

3 Do a solo brainstorming session. Get paper and pencil, and number the paper from 1–

20. In the next two minutes, write down at least 20 things that you could do to thrill customers, not just satisfy them. These ideas don't have to be practical. Assume you have unlimited time and resources. When you're finished, you'll likely find that at least one of your ideas is practical enough to implement soon. And, the ones you thought were wacky as you wrote them, may give you ideas for others that could work.

4 Build a customer database with information about purchasing patterns.

5 Survey your customers to find out what they like and dislike about you and your competitors.

6 Ask customers who else they use for services you could provide. Calculate how much of their business you're getting today. Calculate the lifetime value of the business you're getting and the business you could be getting.

7 Most of all, think how you can make each customer feel special over the long term.

Chapter 7

MARKETING TO YOUR EMPLOYEES WITH INCENTIVES
You Have their Hands, Now Win their Hearts!

Rick Blabolil

Richard A. (Rick) Blabolil is executive vice president of Marketing Innovators International, Inc. and JCPenney Incentive Sales, a full-service division of Marketing Innovators. For 15 years, he has managed various departments at Marketing Innovators, participating in incentive design teams, compensation forums, and advisory boards.

Mr. Blabolil is also president of the Association of Incentive Gift Certificate Suppliers (AIGCS). He was instrumental in the formation of the AIGCS, created in 1995 to increase awareness of gift certificates as a viable option for incentive programs. He was elected to a two-year term as president after serving on the executive board since the Association's inception. In addition to the AIGCS, Mr. Blabolil is involved with a number of industry-related organizations including the Incentive Federation, the American Management Association, and the American Productivity and Quality Center.

Mr. Blabolil earned an MBA from Northwestern University and his undergraduate degree from Iowa State University.

Richard A. Blabolil, Marketing Innovators International, Inc., 9701 West Higgins Road, Rosemont, IL 60018-4717; phone (800) 543-7373, (874) 696-1111; fax (847) 696-3194; e-mail rblaboli@marketinginnovators.com.

Chapter 7

MARKETING TO YOUR EMPLOYEES WITH INCENTIVES
You Have their Hands, Now Win their Hearts!

Rick Blabolil

"You get what you reward."
—Ken Blanchard, *The One Minute Manager*

Incentives are rewards. Incentives can also be motivators. Organizations might use incentive gifts for consumer promotions to encourage purchases and loyalty (for example, airline mileage programs). Businesses can also use incentives for employees to encourage specific behaviors.

The first known incentive program has been traced back to 1902. National Cash Register, the most progressive company of its day, is credited with first using incentives to increase sales.

In addition to trying to increase sales, today's organizations most frequently use employee incentives to improve customer service, productivity, and safety, and to encourage employee suggestions.

Incentives usually involve concrete awards. However, recognition can be more important than the monetary value of the reward. As demonstrated by the Hawthorne studies in the 1950s, performance and productivity gains are made by paying attention to people, acknowledging their contributions, and recognizing their importance— not necessarily by simply increasing the amount of monetary gifts.

THE PURPOSE OF AN INCENTIVE PROGRAM

The business world has undergone many changes over the last twenty years. Mergers, acquisitions, and leveraged buyouts have caused radical restructuring in many companies. Foreign competitors have taken significant amounts of market share and dismantled industries. Cost measures have resulted in substantial downsizing. Technology is changing at an ever-increasing rate. Customers are more demanding regarding the quality of products and services. Employee loyalty has been eroding and traditional human resources practices are being challenged.

In today's changing business environment, there are two ways for organizations to compete. The first is with an external competitive focus where the strategy is to meet or beat other companies.

The second way to compete is through internal improvement and employee empowerment. Here the strategy is for employees to improve and compete with themselves. Empowered employees are passionate about their potential and the organizations's potential. They challenge themselves with questions like:

- What can I do to help the organization reach the goals?
- Where can I improve?
- How good can we be?
- What is our real potential?

> "If you are trying to change the way you run a company, one of the most visible things you have to change is the way you compensate, reward, and recognize people."
> —Paul Allaire,
> CEO, Xerox Corp.

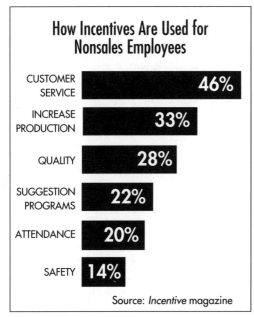

How Incentives Are Used for Nonsales Employees

CUSTOMER SERVICE	46%
INCREASE PRODUCTION	33%
QUALITY	28%
SUGGESTION PROGRAMS	22%
ATTENDANCE	20%
SAFETY	14%

Source: *Incentive* magazine

A company changes as a result of a series of changes initiated by people. Empowered employees contribute their time and ideas for the organization. Employees with an internal competitive focus are neither limited by their competition's successes nor inhibited by their failures.

Incentive programs are an essential part of this focus. An incentive or recognition program focuses messages, expectations, and subsequent efforts. Incentive programs create a climate in which employees successfully motivate themselves.

If an organization dedicates itself to is employees, the employees will dedicate themselves to their customers.

Incentive programs are often used to boost sales because it is so easy to measure sales variables like number of sales, new customers, size of order, and so forth. Smart companies use incentives for their whole team of support people who back up sales. For instance, receptionists at IBM used to get a small part of the commissions on sales.

Incentive programs have spread outside the sales department, and human resources departments now must learn to coordinate programs so they encourage and empower all employees. This chapter will focus on how incentives are used—and can be used—with nonsales employees.

TYPES OF INCENTIVES

Incentives can be anything employees find rewarding. Merchandise, gift certificates, and travel are common incentives. However, incentives can also be symbolic, such as written or verbal recognition, or a trophy.

For instance, a Hewlett-Packard engineer came to his manager with a great idea. The manager knew that immediate reinforcement was important, but the only thing he had on his desk was a banana. So that's what he gave the employee. It started a tradition and now a "golden banana" pin is highly coveted.

Benefits of Incentives

Merchandise and trophies are lasting reminders of appreciation. Travel programs create enduring memories. Furthermore, if the travel incentive award is a group trip where a team of winners travels together, it has the additional benefit of creating a shared team-building experience. This experience usually carries over back to the office and can cut across ranks and departments.

Of course, any well-designed incentive program will more than pay for itself in increased output and profit for the organization. These programs are also a way of sharing the wealth from successes with your employees.

Incentives are a clear form of recognition. They can be used to build teams and to encourage new behaviors. They are also a way for an organization to focus on a particular topic. Strong incentives are a tangible demonstration to employees that there is real organizational commitment to a goal.

> ### Payoffs from Incentives
> Benefits of investments in nonsales employee incentive programs:
> - Edy's Grand Ice Cream reduced inventory 66%, increased productivity 47%, and increased sales volume 830%.
> - Xerox cut new product development time in half.
> - Motorola estimates a $30 increase in earnings for every $1 invested in employee training.
>
> —From an Ernst & Young study for the Labor Department

When Incentives Don't Work

When incentives become entitlements, they generally lose their motivational value. This can happen with a company-wide program where employees receive bonuses that are not tied to specific goals.

When employees receive bonuses just for "showing up," employees who "give their all" begin to resent getting the same reward as those who do the minimum. Charges of favoritism arise when rewards are left up to a superior's judgment. It's best to use a relatively objective scoring system. Incentives can also lose their motivational value when a contest is so easy that everyone counts the reward as part of their regular compensation.

EXAMPLES OF INCENTIVE PROGRAMS

Let's use a very traditional example to illustrate the use of incentives. The selling of cars is the stereotype of old-fashioned, hard-sell selling. As customers rebelled against pushy, high-pressure sales techniques, market share began to go to dealerships that offered a "kinder, gentler approach."

Some auto dealerships changed their sales approaches to soft selling and relationship building. To get that message across—both to their own salespeople and customers—they needed programs that reinforced the point.

To improve customer satisfaction during the sales process and afterwards, one dealership created a survey for salespeople to give customers at various stages of the process. Customer satisfaction became important, even if the customer didn't buy.

Salespeople got rewarded for good ratings, and the rating process continued after the sale. To keep their customers happy, salespeople became customer advocates with the service department. This new emphasis on service increased sales, service department work, and customer satisfaction. And, as discussed in other chapters, high customer satisfaction creates repeat business and referrals—the most profitable kinds of business.

Broader Incentive Programs

We worked with the communications company, Ameritech, to initiate a recognition program for employees throughout the organization. Besides the customer service units, the program included the legal and finance departments, and even the corporate communications division. To implement the program, Ameritech distributed "tool kits" of recognition material to hundreds of managers in their 23 business divisions.

The tool kit included a description of the program for the managers; skill tests for managers to evaluate their recognition efforts; preprinted sticky notes and thank you cards to use for immediate, no-cost recognition; gift certificate forms and catalogs of Ameritech-logoed merchandise; nomination forms for bigger awards;  and Bob Nelson's book *1001 Ways to Reward Employees* for more ideas.

In addition to increasing recognition of employee efforts, the program had a secondary effect. With a kit of material sitting on every manager's desk, and employees hearing what other managers did, it raised interest in the program and put subtle pressure on each manager to actively use the material. The program was a big success and became even bigger the next year.

Multilevel Incentives

To distinguish incentive programs that reward everyone in an organization from the traditional sales-only incentive programs, the new programs are sometimes called "multilevel incentives."

For instance, one company's sales incentive program originally offered incentives only to the sales force. They changed their program to a more balanced one that made the internal support staffers, who were key for service, follow-up, and quality control, eligible for rewards. The reward was six days on the Big Island of Hawaii. When the program ended, 300 employees and spouses, representing all departments, headed off for a great trip that further reinforced the message that all units were part of the same team.

Another example is a nationwide accounting services company that had high client turnover. The company set up a program to increase client satisfaction ratings by 10 percent and client retention by 20 percent. They rewarded nonsales employees for suggestions and client relationship building. The program focused employee attention on these important issues. It improved customer quality ratings by 14 percent and retention by 21.6 percent. Along the way, employee suggestions saved the company $2.3 million nationally!

Low-Cost Employee Rewards

- photos on bulletin board of outstanding performers
- handwritten thank you notes
- special delivery of balloons or flowers
- a special parking place
- recognition in the company newsletter

INCENTIVES CAN WORK FOR YOU

I'm excited about the future use of incentives—particularly for nonsales employees—for three reasons. First, a recent study by the Incentive Federation estimated that only about 26 percent of all companies use *any* form of incentives. And for companies with fewer than ten employees, the number was only five percent. Small companies often think that they can't afford incentives. But statistics show that incentives pay for themselves from 2 to10 times over their cost. Over 90 percent of small businesses aren't taking advantage of incentives to improve their businesses.

Second, only about 10 percent of companies have *any* incentive system for nonsales employees. Nonsales employees represent the majority of employees in any company, so when strong multilevel incentive programs are implemented, the payoffs will be even bigger.

Third, the biggest potential yet is for sales and marketing incentives for nonsales and marketing employees. (Most current programs for nonsales employees offer incentives for improvements in productivity, attendance, or safety.) Marketing-oriented programs are few and far between. Yet *Incentive* magazine says that the few companies that do reward nonsales employees for aiding sales efforts report:

- increased revenues as employees generate more new sales leads than the sales force can handle
- greater loyalty and commitment because employees feel they have a vested interest in results
- better customer service from enthusiastic employees

> "The deepest principle in human nature is the craving to be appreciated"
> —William James

> "Encouragement is oxygen to the soul."
> —George M. Adams

THE FUTURE OF INCENTIVES: NONSALES EMPLOYEES

The fastest growing area of incentives is in the nonsales area. It's exciting that all employees are now gaining opportunities to be recognized and earn incentives.

Promise Makers vs. Promise Keepers

An important and much overlooked issue in most organizations is that the people who make the promises to prospects and customers are usually not the people who have to fulfill them!

Marketing and sales employees make promises to customers, whether directly or through advertising, publicity, and so forth. They are the "promise makers."

The "promise keepers" are everyone else in the company—whether in customer service, manufacturing, research, or shipping. These promise-keeper employees all affect the delivery of the product or service to the customer.

When research and marketing personnel don't get along, it affects delivery of service to the customer. When customer service isn't told when new ads will generate calls, it hurts service to the customer. When management's philosophy isn't supportive of internal service providers, it hurts the customer.

This is a long way of saying that incentives should reward everyone who supports customers. To deliver great customer service, everyone in a company should be aligned to serve customers. Used correctly, incentives have the power to create that alignment between different organizational units.

Many of these new programs are aimed at customer service and teams of employees, because providing great service is a team effort.

Applying Traditional Programs to Nonsales Marketing Efforts

The most common way to use incentives to involve nonsales and marketing employees in generating business is to provide rewards for cross-selling, referrals, and so forth. For instance, tellers in a bank had a program to earn reward points. Points could come from customer satisfaction ratings, from referring customers to other bank services (cross-selling), and from nominations by other employees for exceptional behavior.

Here's an example of how customer service reps can contribute in a big way to sales by supporting referral sources. It was so successful that it won a Gold Key Award from the Incentive Manufacturers Representatives Association.

A Bank of America division aimed a promotion at 1,135 manufactured-home retailers who were their top loan referral sources. A Bank of America customer service rep talked to each retailer to calculate how many loans they would have to refer to win awards, based on the size of their businesses. These customer service employees were helping the referrers, rather than selling. There were several reminders and personal contacts over the course of the program encouraging the dealers.

Final loan volume increased 48 percent for the six-month period of the awards program. And the personal attention also built relationships for the future. Most reps enjoyed helping the people with whom they worked to win awards.

More Examples

Rewarding everyone in the company for increased sales is a common program. Here are two similar examples of traditional sales incentive programs applied in a nontraditional setting. Two different finance companies— Beneficial and American General—wanted to increase the number of loans. They had theme contests where branch managers, district managers, and employees could all win prizes (the top prizes were trips to Hawaii).

More Ways Banks Reward Employees

At the Bank of Boston, employees award each other gold stars when they observe each other give great service or go beyond the call of duty. The stars earned are displayed publicly and are coveted by staff. It's pure recognition at no cost. You can also get stars if customers compliment your service.

First Chicago Bank has a four-level recognition program to encourage great service.

(1) Informal peer recognition. Your good internal or external service is recognized.

(2) A peer fills out a nomination form to recognize your performance.

(3) Individuals are selected from the nominated group to be recognized as elite service givers with a plaque.

(4) There is an event to recognize the elite and one is selected as the service provider of the year, with a certificate and prizes.

The contest period created excitement and got everyone pulling together since most prizes depended on branch office total production.

Theme-based promotions give a recognizable style to a kickoff party, updates, and small prizes from the home office. For instance, when employees of one of the finance companies opened a box of party items, a light-sensitive chip made party sounds. At the other company, everyone was given sunglasses to remind them of Hawaii. Both programs were successful with loans up 34 percent and 27 percent respectively.

MORE WAYS TO INVOLVE EVERYONE IN MARKETING

There are many less traditional ways to use incentive programs for nonsales employees.

Even employees who don't contact customers directly can make a big difference. For example, in the warehouse of Smith and Hawken (a catalog garden supplies company), a mispacked order costs a lot in returns and customer dissatisfaction. So, a simple program was instituted. For every day with no mispacked orders or customer returns, the company put a small amount—less than $5—in a kitty. Mispacked orders and customer complaints dropped by 95 percent. And at the end of the month, the workers spent the $75 to $100 that had accumulated on a pizza party.

Here's an example of simple marketing effort by a nonmarketing employee from *1001 Ways to Market Your Services* by Rick Crandall. A printing company driver helps generate sales leads. Whenever he delivers a customer's order, he goes to the businesses on either side of the customer and asks for the business card of the person who buys printing. (If he can talk to the print buyer directly, he collects more information.) He then delivers these cards to the sales department and receives a commission on any orders generated from his leads. In an average day, the driver collects 10–20 leads for the sales force.

Employees as Researchers, and More

Research is an important, but often overlooked, part of marketing. Unless you know who your customers are, what your customers want, who your competitors are, and the like, you can't operate efficiently.

If you're in the research department of a company that sells to busy professionals, it can be hard to gather information. Most people are tired of surveys. And it's even harder to get professionals to give up $100 worth of their time to answer your questions. A pharmaceutical company used Sony gift certificates and a catalog of CDs to get a record number of completed questionnaires from doctors. The novelty and the value got their attention and got the needed answers for product development and marketing.

Here is a "James Bond" undercover approach to market research. One printing delivery driver would observe the other printing jobs sitting on the loading dock as he unloaded his truck. He would write down the names of the printers and the type of jobs and give them to the sales force. The sales force would follow up and let the customers know about their capacities in those areas. Often the customers said they

Analyze Your Competitors

An even more unusual example of a research contribution could come from your accounting department. There is a speciality called "forensic accounting." These experts analyze the public filings of competitors in light of what they know about costs in the industry. They are able to produce information about profits by product lines of competitors. Perhaps your accounting staff could make estimates like this. Or, in a less competitive direction, perhaps they could help your customers analyze their costs so they could better utilize your products and services.

hadn't realized that the company did that kind of work.

Another form of marketing research is the "mystery customer." Here you hire services to shop in your store (or call you or your competitors) and rate how they were treated. All your employees could fill this function. What if you gave each one a small budget to shop a competitor? They'd collect information, feel involved, and perhaps even have a little fun.

INVOLVING STAFF IN CUSTOMER INCENTIVES

As a consumer, you probably participate in a customer loyalty program. The best known are airline mileage awards where every time you fly on a particular airline, you receive points towards free trips. Some charge cards give you rebates for spending. On the local side, many retailers give customers cards that are punched with each purchase, with a completed card redeemable for a free product.

Help Customers Win

Here's a new area for employee involvement in incentives. Rather than rewarding employees for sales, reward them for helping customers benefit from incentive programs.

Let's start with an example of industrial customers. Every year in America, billions of dollars in "co-op advertising" are offered to retailers by their suppliers. Typical programs offer to match advertising dollars in the local media.

Many of these dollars go unused every year. Sometimes the programs are too complicated. If advertising salespeople kept up on available co-op dollars and did all the work for retailers to take advantage of them, they would be providing a real service. The retailers get free advertising they would have missed—and the salespeople sell more advertising. This is exactly what smart radio stations and other media do.

Take this same idea and apply it to your customers, whether end users or distributors. If you offer programs to customers that aren't being utilized, involve your customer service and other employees in notifying customers of opportunities they are missing. These shouldn't be sales calls. They should be "giving away free money calls"—for instance, notifying customers that they are eligible for an award or a rebate, but must apply for it by a certain date.

> ... you now qualify for our "Star Customer" discounts...

Usually these loyalty programs are set up to motivate customers to do more of something. And that's as far as most companies take it. But when you tell customers who don't know that they qualify for something, you turn it into a bonus reward program. It's an acknowledgment that they are important to you, even when it costs you something. You exceed their expectations.

GUIDELINES FOR SUCCESSFUL INCENTIVE PROGRAMS

If you decide to offer incentive programs for your staff, we've found these points to be helpful to keep in mind:

1. Pick goals that are a stretch, but are achievable. Research on achievement motivation, and our experience, says that if a goal is too hard, it will demotivate rather than motivate.

2. Don't "grade on a curve." Don't create internal competition where most people lose and only a few win. If everyone achieves the objectives, everyone should win.

3. Support teamwork. Even in sales contests, good support is necessary to fulfill orders. Reward the team if it is a team effort.

4. Don't drag it out. Quarterly goals are probably as long as you should go without rewards. When the total program is longer, institute intermediate goals.

5. Recognition is important. Not everyone is motivated by the same rewards. But everyone appreciates being recognized for a job well done.

6. Don't hesitate to get help. For example, services like ours, that show you what is possible, can pay for themselves—or even save you money—by increasing productivity.

THE FUTURE OF INCENTIVE PROGRAMS

In the area of general incentives, new technologies will allow much closer tracking of individual customer buying habits.

However, there are two main points I'd like to leave you with. First, simple applications of incentives have been proven for years to be cost effective and can benefit any business. Second, sales-type incentives can be very useful for nonsales and marketing employees. Start simply by rewarding something you want to encourage. Then build from there.

One-to-One Marketing

"High tech now makes high touch even more possible. Instead of 'targeting' groups of customers who share characteristics in common in order to serve them better, you can now reach out personally to each customer by creating a custom offer only for them."

—Don Peppers and Martha Rogers,
The One To One Future: Building Relationships One Customer at a Time

ACTION SUMMARY

"The friction of activity strengthens and enlarges life."

—Robert Louis Stevenson

1 Discuss with employees what sorts of incentives they would be interested in.

2 Detail the kinds of behaviors you'd like to encourage, such as great customer service.

3 Benchmark your current customer service with a simple survey.

4 Pick a simple incentive program to start. For example, train peers to recognize each other's achievements.

5 Improve communication between your promise makers (the sales force) and your promise keepers (everyone else).

6 Consider a theme promotion where everyone has the opportunity to win prizes for good performance.

Chapter 8

THE MAGIC OF A MARKETING SYSTEM

Theodore W. Garrison III

Theodore W. Garrison III is a professional speaker and consultant. His programs to corporations, associations, and other organizations focus on marketing and business management strategies. As an advocate of Michael Gerber's E-Myth philosophy, his presentations emphasize how to take charge of your business and your life.

He has more than 20 years of business, leadership, and motivation experience working in the real estate development industry, where he held executive positions involved with the design, construction, and marketing of almost a billion dollars worth of construction, including hotels, office buildings, and public facilities. He has been a licensed real estate broker since 1981.

In 1994, he established Garrison Associates which provides seminars and keynote speeches for businesses and associations on marketing and management strategies.

Mr. Garrison is a member of the National Speakers Association and the American Seminar Leaders Association.

Theodore W. Garrison III, Garrison Associates, 900 W. Valley Road, Suite 201H, Wayne, PA 19087; phone (610) 341-8605; fax (610) 889-0901; e-mail: garrison@bellatlantic.net.

Chapter 8

THE MAGIC OF A MARKETING SYSTEM

Theodore W. Garrison III

"Drive your business, or it will drive thee."
—Ben Franklin

There is no magic formula or trick that will make your marketing challenges disappear. On the other hand, a well-run marketing system can be so effective that the results might seem like magic. This chapter will reveal how to make your marketing more effective—and more enjoyable—through the use of a system.

SYSTEMS MAKE THINGS EASIER

The reason for implementing a marketing system is simple. If marketing isn't easy or enjoyable, you won't do it. You'll always find justifications to postpone your marketing efforts. But, "later" is frequently too late. A good marketing system allows you to organize everyone's efforts and put them on automatic pilot while insuring the process stays on course. With such a system in place, you will only have to check in occasionally to make any necessary mid-flight adjustments.

The primary objective of this chapter is to explain how a marketing system operates. However, equally important is demonstrating how people who don't like marketing—or don't think marketing is their responsibility—can use a marketing system to make their efforts more enjoyable while at the same time improving their effectiveness. But before you can develop a marketing system, your business has to have a focus, so let's begin there.

MARKETING FOCUS: POSITIONING AND USP

When Domino's Pizza was started, the founders didn't worry about whether or not they made the best pizza. Their business concept was to deliver an edible pizza in less than 30 minutes or give it to the customer free of charge. The founders clearly understood that when people order a pizza, they want it immediately. So they marketed Domino's as the quick-delivery pizza.

The Domino's story illustrates two fundamental marketing concepts: *unique selling proposition* (USP) and *positioning.* These two concepts are critical to the development of an effective marketing system. Even if you hire someone to plan and implement your marketing program, you will first need to develop these two concepts. These concepts tell you where you're going.

Simply stated, your USP is what makes you or your business unique from others in the same business. Without a USP, you can't distinguish yourself from the competition. In Domino's case, their USP was their promise to deliver within 30 minutes or you get a free pizza.

In contrast, positioning is how your customers and prospects perceive your company, service,

"If you don't know where you're going, you are likely to end up someplace else."
—Casey Stengel

A Few of the Many Ways to Position a Pizza Restaurant

or product. Positioning includes USP and its impact on the prospect's mind.

One of the most powerful positioning strategies is to be the first one in a category. Domino's was positioned as the first to promise quick delivery of pizza. Many times, when a company introduces a new product, they create a new category that becomes identified with their brand name (for example, people ask for Scotch tape, not cellophane tape; a Xerox copy, not a plain paper, electrostatic copy; a Kleenex, not a tissue; Jello, not gelatin).

For more information on finding a unique position, I suggest you read one or more of the books written by Al Ries and Jack Trout. The titles include, *Positioning, The 22 Immutable Laws of Marketing, The New Positioning,* and *Focus.*

> "Positioning is what you do to the mind of the prospect. It's how they see you compared to their alternatives."
>
> —Al Ries and Jack Trout; *Positioning: The Battle for Your Mind*

A MARKETING SYSTEM

In his book, *The E-Myth Revisited,* Michael E. Gerber expresses the philosophy that, for a business to be successful, all its activities must be duplicable. This is the concept of the modern franchise. The idea behind creating a system is that every task can be easily duplicated, so anyone can do it. And, when tasks are duplicable every time, then the results are predictable every time.

To achieve this state of predictable results, Gerber says that the foundation of the marketing process must consist of three distinct activities: *innovation, quantification,* and *orchestration.*

Every successful marketing system undergoes revisions in response to changing market conditions. This requires *innovation*, followed by *quantification* of the results to determine if the innovation was an improvement. When the data collected indicate the innovation is an improvement, the innovation must be implemented in the business' operations. This activity is called *orchestration*. Successful businesses repeat this process over and over in a never-ending quest to find the best way to conduct every aspect of their businesses.

Marketing Is More

Too often, people think of marketing only as direct sales or advertising. This could not be further from the truth. The best definition I have ever heard of marketing is from Harvard professor Michael Porter: "Marketing is anything you do to get or keep a customer." Michael Gerber elaborates by saying, "The entire process by which the business does business is a marketing tool, a mechanism for finding and keeping customers." In order to stand out from competitors, this makes innovation the key to any marketing system.

INNOVATION

Innovation involves the creation of ideas, but more importantly, the implementation of those ideas. Harvard professor Theodore Levitt states in his book *Marketing for Business Growth,* "Creativity thinks up new things. Innovation does new things." Since marketing is about satisfying customers, marketing innovation is about finding new ways to satisfy the needs of customers. Whether your job title includes sales and marketing or not, you should contribute to uncovering and satisfying customer needs.

LensCrafters' Position: Speed

Some of the most successful businesses are noted for their innovations which benefit customers. An example is LensCrafters' service approach.

When LensCrafters was started, the founders asked consumers what their biggest complaints were about the process of obtaining eye glasses.

The answer was time: Several trips to the doctor were required, followed by weeks of delay in obtaining new eyeglasses.

The founders concluded that a great marketing strategy would be to provide new glasses in an hour or less. Once they had the idea, they worked on finding a way to do it. Their solution was to move the laboratory into the location where the eye glasses were sold. Their innovation had an unbelievable marketing impact on their business.

> "Many businesses can use speed of operations and service as a competitive advantage today."
> —Tom Peters

Don't Say, "May I Help You?"

It is not necessary to create major innovations, as did LensCrafters and Domino's. Often, simple changes can produce big results. As an example of the value of setting up a system for everything, Michael Gerber tells the following story about retail selling.

> When you go into a retail store, the first question clerks usually ask is, "May I help you?" That leads to the answer, "No, thank you, I'm just looking." This dialogue is costing retailers thousands of dollars in sales. Studies indicate that if you change the store employee's initial question to "Hi, have you been in the store before?" sales will go up between 10 percent and 16 percent immediately. Why? Regardless

of whether the shopper answers yes or no, you respond that you have a new special program for new or repeat shoppers, as the case may be, and you offer to take a moment to explain it. Of course, you will need to have some kind of program, but that should not be too difficult.

Fit Methods to Your Style

If you are concerned about your creative ability in developing new marketing innovations for your business, there are several books that can be of assistance. One I recommend is Jay Levinson's book, *Guerrilla Marketing Weapons,* where Levinson describes 100 affordable marketing methods. His diverse list includes such weapons as: pricing, distribution, business cards, contests, attire, service, follow-up, clubs and associations, written articles, talks, newsletters, hours of operation, developing credibility, signage, consultations, and booths in malls, to name a few. He offers something for everyone. Other books are listed in the references. The goal is to find marketing methods that fit in with your business operations and that you find both enjoyable and effective.

Your next question might be, "How did someone figure out that sales went up 16 percent by changing the store's greeting?" or "How do I know which marketing innovations will work for me?" The answer brings us to the second activity in the marketing system—quantification.

> ### Creative Marketing
>
> "A jeweler attracted attention and customers by inventing outlandishly expensive gifts like a miniature hourglass with real diamonds instead of sand. He hardly sold any, but attracted national publicity and sales of his more conventional pieces soared."
>
> —Jay Conrad Levinson, *Guerrilla Marketing*

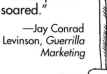

QUANTIFICATION

It is essential to track the effects of everything you do, so you know what works and what doesn't in terms of getting and keeping customers. If you keep working on your business to make it better, you will continue to try innovations. But when you attempt these innovations, you must quantify them to make sure you obtain the desired results. This process applies equally to the one-person business.

Remember the 80–20 Rule

According to the 80–20 rule, 20% of the things you do generate 80% of the results. Therefore, your aim is to concentrate on the most effective 20%. But the only way for you to know which tasks are in the 20% category is to measure the results of everything you do.

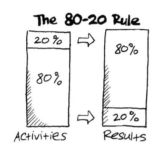

The 80-20 Rule

Getting Started on a Quantification System

If you don't already have a marketing system, begin by identifying how you perform all your marketing-related activities. You may be surprised to learn that you don't have a set way of doing them. That's okay. Simply select one of your ways of doing each task and establish that method as your base. Once you have measured the performance of your base method, you can try one of your other methods to test its results. At this point, it is easy to select the best method and toss out the other. Continue this process until you have reduced each of your marketing tasks to a single method. This approach will leave you with your best method for each marketing task you perform.

Experiment with New Methods

Now you are ready to introduce innovations into your marketing system. For example, if you want to try a new greeting with customers, you can measure it against the performance of your current greeting. If your sales improve, continue to use the new greeting. However, if your sales drop, return to your original greeting. In this manner, you can continuously try new innovations and quickly determine if they are improvements or not.

Test New Procedure

SALES DOWN   SALES UP

KEEP NEW PROCEDURES

SALES DECLINE   SALES CONTINUE TO RISE

RETURN TO STANDARD PROCEDURE   CONTINUE TO USE NEW PROCEDURES

Using quantification is the only way to determine if your innovations are an improvement for customers. It doesn't matter what you think; it only matters what customers think. For example, when BMW, which was known for selling the "ultimate driving machine," decided to broaden its market and pursue the large Mercedes market, BMW created a problem for itself. Namely, how can a large car be the ultimate driving machine? The new product destroyed the company's focus in the mind of the consumer and sales began to drop off. The public didn't buy into the innovation.

The next activity—orchestration—involves implementing the successful innovations.

ORCHESTRATION

Michael Gerber says, "Orchestration is the elimination of discretion, or choice, at the operating level of your business." This means that once you determine the best way to greet your customers, you then have everybody address your customers that way.

A major factor in McDonald's success is that everybody knows exactly what kind of hamburger

and fries they will receive regardless of the McDonald's they enter.

Have you wondered how Ray Kroc managed to get teenagers in California, Illinois, Florida, and Maine to produce the exact same fry? It is really quite simple. McDonald's starts with the same kind of potato. Each potato is cut into fries of the same size. At all locations, the fries are cooked in the same type of oil in the same type of fryer at exactly the same temperature for exactly the same amount of time. Is there any surprise that all the fries come out exactly the same?

While at first glance, the cooking of french fries may appear to be an operational issue; in this case, it is also part of the marketing effort. A consistent product is part of McDonald's positioning—what they stand for.

The Power of Orchestration

The real power of orchestration is that when you can assure the same performance each and every time, you own it. McDonald's owns their hamburgers, french fries, and other food products because everyone who has ever eaten at a McDonald's knows exactly what the food will be like regardless of who is doing the cooking. As a result of this predictability, people choose to eat at McDonald's rather than taking a risk with an unknown, or less familiar, restaurant.

Now, keeping the McDonald's experience in mind, think about your typical experience when dealing with most small businesses. Usually you're lucky if you get *any* consistency, even if you deal with the same person on a day-to-day basis. Customers desire predictability in what they purchase. We all resist change to some degree. As consumers, we don't want to encounter interactions and procedures that are randomly different every time we seek a product or service.

Continuous Improvement

Predictability and innovation do not contradict each other. The quest for excellence is a never-ending journey, not a destination. In order to have a great business, you must always strive to be better.

In a system, one innovation at a time is tested so that the results can be quantified. McDonald's tests new products all the time—popular ones are added to the menu and unpopular ones dropped (remember McRib?). But they test one item at a time. You'll never have the experience of walking into a McDonald's and being confronted by a totally unfamiliar menu.

> "Other people owned McDonald's franchises before I did. What set us apart was the consistent use of clear systems and standards."
> —Ray Kroc, *Grinding It Out*

Systems Increase Freedom

Developing a marketing system will give you a new sense of freedom from your business. By developing a marketing system you are beginning to work *on* your business, instead of *in* it. Michael Gerber says that working on the business "is the heart of the process: not efficiency, not effectiveness, not more money, not to 'downsize,' or 'get lean,' but to simply and finally create more life for everyone who comes into contact with the business, but most of all, for you, the person who owns it."

Increasing your freedom is the real magic of the system, which leads us to the next topic—making your marketing effort fun.

MAKING YOUR MARKETING FUN

At this point, I'm sure some of you are thinking, "I thought this book was for people who aren't in marketing, or maybe don't even like it. This marketing system stuff seems like a lot of work." In the beginning, a system does take extra effort, but the long-term benefits are huge.

What most people mean when they say they don't like marketing is that they don't like making cold calls and other personal sales. The benefit of a system is that you can determine the most effective ways to market your business so that it fits your personal style. Through systematic innovation, quantification, and orchestration, you can achieve even better results than through cold calls and direct sales.

EXAMPLES OF MARKETING SYSTEMS

The next chapter has more details on implementing a marketing plan. Here are a few examples to get you started.

- A cosmetic surgeon who specializes in keeping the rich and famous looking young and glamorous has developed a USP that distinguishes him from other cosmetic surgeons. He is a good surgeon who knows how to pamper his patients by catering to their physical and emotional needs. He has a waiting lists for his services, despite his very high fees. How does he do this? Through repeat business and the use of referrals, the most powerful marketing tools. (See Chapter 4 for more on customer service.)

Systems Encourage Creativity

Some people think that using a system restricts their creativity. Not so! A system lets you control the routine work so you can unlease your creativity.

- I have met several successful professional speakers who claim they don't do any marketing. Sorry, but they are wrong. Because if they were not marketing their services, how would anyone know they existed? What they meant was that they don't make cold calls or do direct mailings to obtain business. Then, how do they market their services? First, by providing an extraordinary performance on the stage, which is what they wanted to do in the first place. Secondly, they cater to the needs of their clients and, as a result, build a network of people who need their services. Networking is another of the great marketing strategies. (See Chapter 3 for more examples of networking.)

- The final example is about a real estate broker friend of mine. John specializes in leasing office space. Over time, John established himself as "the expert" on the local office leasing market. How did he do this? He learned the market, then he published a quarterly newsletter on local office leasing, which he sent to all property owners and prospective tenants. The result is that, even when John isn't the listing agent on a particular property, prospective tenants call John because of his recognized expertise to make sure they are getting the best deal. John then gets the opportunity to present his properties to the prospect—a real business advantage.

Systematized Real Estate Sales

One of the most productive real estate agents in the country—who did $40 million in yearly sales—was distinguished by his powerful marketing systems. His listing presentation was contained in a custom book that covered every point precisely. He created a direct mail program to mail to prospects on a specific schedule, and coordinated with services like coupon-mailer Val-Pak to handle all the work. He also set up systems for alloting his time and delegating work.

WHO ARE YOU? WHAT DOES YOUR COMPANY REPRESENT?

> "All purchase decisions, all repurchase decisions, hinge, ultimately, on conversations and relationships....All dealings are personal dealings in the end."
>
> —Tom Peters

To create a successful business, it is essential that people associate you with a specific USP. An even better situation is for you to position yourself so that you come to mind when your customers and prospects think of a particular class of service or product.

What the three prior examples have in common is that in each case the principals of the businesses established themselves prominently in the minds of prospects by how they conducted their businesses. When people need their services, their names immediately come to mind. Accomplish this for your business, and you will enjoy doing your marketing, because you will be doing what you want to do.

SUMMARY

Finding what you enjoy about marketing may not come immediately, especially if marketing is not your main job. But, by setting up a system that works for you, your success is only a matter of time.

Some approaches work better with business-to-business sales and others work better with business-to-consumer sales. By trying new things (innovation), tracking their effects (quantification), and applying the best results in a system (orchestration), your marketing will work for you rather than you working for your marketing.

Your goal is to match your personality and business to the marketing strategies that will work best for you. When you do this, marketing will be fun—and effective.

Good luck.

ACTION SUMMARY

"My dreams were always linked to some form of action."

—Ray Kroc, McDonald's

1 What is your unique sales proposition? Make a list of all the benefits you (or your organization) offer. Then, go through the list and cross off any benefits also offered by your competition. Any of the remaining benefits can be used as your USP. (Remember, *you* can be a benefit. Your past experience can be a benefit—for example, an accountant who has worked for the IRS. Your personality can be a benefit—the only dentist in town who sings to his patients or performs at comedy clubs and tells jokes to his patients.)

2 Survey your employees and customers, either formally or informally, to see if they understand USP—and whether they position your organization where you think it is. If there's a discrepancy, it's time to reposition yourself.

3 Write a plan to try new marketing techniques in your business (innovation).

4 Plan how you will measure the results of each new experiment (quantification).

5 Get your marketing procedures in writing (orchestration). If marketing procedures are not currently written down, ask your employees to write down the procedures they use. You'll end up with several different versions from which you can piece together a good plan. The different strategies will also provide ideas for future testing.

Chapter 9

HOW TO BUILD A MARKETING MACHINE

Christian Frederiksen

Christian (Chris) Frederiksen is an accomplished speaker, seminar leader, and consult-ant. His specialty is working with professionals—particularly accountants and lawyers—to develop effective marketing programs and management systems. In his worldwide practice, he targets individuals and firms that want to make more money and have more fun.

Chris Frederiksen draws from 30 years' experience as a marketer and provider of professional services. He has been a partner in two international CPA consulting firms and also built one of the largest independent firms in California. He is currently managing partner of Frederiksen & Co., a firm of CPAs and management consultants in Mill Valley, California.

Mr. Frederiksen is the author of a number of books and tape programs, including *How to Build a Million Dollar Practice* and *How to Manage a Million Dollar Practice*. His latest book is *The Marketing Correspondence Cookbook: A Collection of Sure-fire Marketing Letters (and other Recipes) for the Practicing Accountant.*

Christian Frederiksen, Frederiksen & Co., CPAs, Inc., 333 Miller Avenue, Mill Valley, CA 94941; phone (415) 389-1099; fax (415) 383-5836; e-mail chrisf@ frederiksen.com; www.frederiksen.com.

Chapter 9

HOW TO BUILD A MARKETING MACHINE

Christian Frederiksen

"A good plan implemented today is better than a perfect plan implemented tomorrow."
—George Patton

To build a thriving business in today's competitive business environment, *everyone* needs to be involved in marketing. Everyone—from receptionist to CEO—must contribute to generating leads and prospects.

So, what stops us from marketing?

If you operate a business, you have been tempted at one time or another to cut back on marketing, "until things pick up." Yet we all know that a steady stream of new work is the lifeblood of any business and the only way to ensure long-term success and profitability.

Many people are scared off from marketing by confusing it with selling. While there must be as many definitions of marketing as there are books on the subject, I am defining it here to mean everything you do in your business to generate prospects. This is contrasted with selling, which I consider to be the process of converting a prospect into a paying client.

If you already have full-time responsibilities in, say, a technical or line function, it's easy to avoid marketing. After all, business is getting busier and the work week is getting longer. As Chapter 1 noted, you can rationalize why you're not doing it:

- I don't have time!
- It's not my responsibility!
- I tried it and it didn't work!
- I'm not good at it!

This chapter will show you how to build your own "marketing machine." This engine will generate lots of new business for you. And, new business makes organizations prosper and grow — whether you're profit or nonprofit.

Let's look at the typical components of an effective marketing program:

- clear focus
- referral development system
- good marketing materials
- direct mail and phone follow-up
- public relations
- newsletters

Are You a Cost Center or a Profit Center?

This is the question that is routinely asked by corporations today as they reengineer their work forces. To be perceived as a key member of the business who is truly adding value, you need to be perceived as a marketeer as well as a skilled professional or technician.

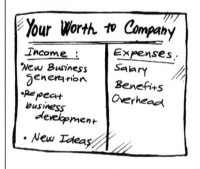

CLEAR FOCUS

Firms today need to be crystal clear as to what they do and who they serve. Taking whatever business happens to come in the door doesn't result in high profitability and will cause problems with resource allocation, your stress level, and quality control.

Rating Your Business

Think in terms of focusing your business both by product/service and by industry/profession.

Here's a useful exercise.

First, make a list of the principal products and services that you offer. Second, make a list of the principal industries or professions that you serve. Next, plot each of the above items on a grid such as the one pictured below.

On the bottom (horizontal axis), determine the expected growth for each industry or profession. For example, software developers are high growth, whereas independent automobile dealers are low growth. On the vertical axis, determine how easy it will be for you to increase market share—for example, attracting software developer clients may be relatively easy because there are a lot of them, the industry is fragmented, and no particular firm selling to them has dominance. On the other hand, you may conclude that increasing market share among new car dealers would be difficult.

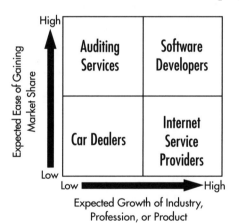

Expected Growth of Industry, Profession, or Product

Now, do the same for your products and services. Let's say, for example, that you run an accounting firm. You may conclude that providing auditing services is low growth, although it may be easy to gain market share by aggressive pricing. Financial services may be both high growth and easy to market.

This exercise tells you where to focus your marketing effort—namely the top right-hand quadrant (high growth plus easy entry). By focusing your energy on offering the right things—to the right groups—your marketing will be much more successful.

REFERRAL DEVELOPMENT SYSTEM

Most of your new business will come from referrals, both from your current customers and from other sources. In order to get referrals, you have to ask for them. This means frequent contact with customers, "centers of influence," and friends.

The best way to stimulate regular referrals is to set up a systematic lunch program. You and your colleagues should each

Never Say "Busy"

Never tell anyone, "I'm busy." That's the quickest way to drive away a prospect or dry up a referral source. Instead, say (with great enthusiasm), "Business is great...and I'm looking for more!"

"How's business?"   "Great."

go to lunch three times a week with people who can send you business and make introductions. It may take several months for this program to show results, so be patient. While you're waiting, you'll meet a lot of interesting people and make some new friends. Organizations that have a structured lunch program attract a lot of good customers over the long term. If lunch isn't a good time in your industry for a get-together, then do breakfast or dinner.

GOOD MARKETING MATERIALS

The written and printed information you send out is your personal ambassador. First impressions count, so you want your materials to convey exactly the right image. Basic marketing gear includes a brochure (the simpler the better) and, depending on your business, various booklets or specification sheets promoting specific services or the industries that you serve.

Your Image

Review your printed materials regularly to make sure they are current and consistent. If you don't have a company logo, get one that is colorful and distinctive.

Before you sit down with a graphic designer to develop your logo and organizational "look," do this exercise. First, list 10 adjectives that people now use about your firm or about people in your industry (these should be positive or neutral adjectives rather than pejorative ones). Next, list 10 adjectives that you *would like* people to use about you.

We did this exercise recently with the staff of a law firm—this is the result:

Current Adjectives	Desired Adjectives
1. Conservative	1. Proactive
2. Accurate	2. Approachable
3. Forthright	3. Caring
4. Competent	4. Trustworthy
5. Thoughtful	5. Communicative
6. Expensive	6. Responsive
7. Diligent	7. Professional
8. Professional	8. Imaginative
9. Learned	9. Timely
10. Thorough	10. Consistent

This information was extremely helpful to the firm's graphics specialist in developing appropriate marketing materials and designing a firm logo.

Live Up to Your Literature

The adjectives in your "Desired" list must accurately reflect your business—if they don't, your literature can backfire. If you promise "timely" responses in your brochure, make sure you live up to that promise.

The list of desired adjectives can be made into a poster (as small as business-card size) that can be placed around the office. Keeping these desired characteristics in front of employees motivates them to live up to expectations.

WE ARE:

CARING
FAST
HELPFUL
PROACTIVE

Distributing Your Marketing Materials

Once you have produced basic marketing literature, develop a distribution plan. Here's a sample one that you can modify to meet your needs:

1. Send two copies of each item to clients and referral sources. Ask them to pass along the second copy to someone who needs your services.

2. Set out a display of materials in your reception area and make sure that your receptionist keeps everything current and tidy.

3. Keep a supply of materials with you, and make sure your employees do the same.

4. If you get the opportunity to make a speech, distribute your materials to each participant beforehand (by putting a brochure on each chair, for example). That way, the audience members are familiar with you and your products before you start talking and will be more responsive to what you say.

5. Include marketing literature with each piece of correspondence, both to your clients and prospects.

Make a Kit to Help Your Customers and Prospects

Many firms would do well to produce some kind of kit that can be used as a "freebie." A freebie is something that:

- people want;
- provides valuable information; and
- you are willing to give away.

Here are some examples:

Computer Company. Basic Systems Kit, explaining various systems and how they are configured, avoiding problems, maintenance, backup, checklists, etc. This could include a free disk with shareware, virus protection programs, etc.

CPA Firm. New Business Kit, explaining setting up books, payroll and sales taxes, income taxes, etc.

Insurance Broker. A kit explaining the different forms of insurance, what various terms mean, avoiding claims, risk management, etc.

The Internet

Being on the Internet is now a requirement as more and more clients use e-mail instead of letters or faxes.

From a marketing perspective, it is helpful (and impressive) to have your own Web site, which you can develop for a surprisingly small outlay. In most communities, you can find a Web site developer, who will charge you a few hundred dollars for a simple Web site.

Do not expect major marketing results from having a Web site—but it's important to be perceived as a "cutting-edge" firm. You can visit our Web site @ www.frederiksen.com.

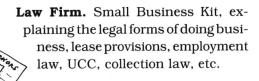

Law Firm. Small Business Kit, explaining the legal forms of doing business, lease provisions, employment law, UCC, collection law, etc.

Your Niche Focus

If you serve a particular kind of client, you can customize a kit to their industry to demonstrate your expertise.

Once you have produced such a kit, you can give it as a "freebie" to a wide variety of people, including:

- Respondents to your direct mail—preferably delivered in person.
- New clients—they will be impressed by your organization and concern.
- Existing clients—this can be a catalyst for a discussion of additional services.
- Referral sources—multiple copies with a request that they be distributed.
- Visitors to your office—put copies in the reception area for people to look at while they wait.

In addition to the marketing materials identified so far, specialty advertising gimmicks have also become popular (pens, pencils, golf balls, and the like). It sometimes seems that the tackier they are, the more clients like them—there's no accounting for taste!

DIRECT MAIL AND PHONE FOLLOW-UP

With good marketing materials in place, it's time to reach out.

Direct mail is the cornerstone of a promotional marketing program. Combined with phone follow-up, it is a very effective way to generate appointments with prospective clients. Our firm sends out an average of 100 letters per week which results in four or five new clients.

Three ingredients are essential to making your direct mail marketing effective:

1. **Enthusiasm!** This must come through in every letter, every phone call, and every meeting.

2. **Time.** Direct mail marketing is a long-term process requiring a real commitment. It may take a while to get your direct mail program fully operational and effective. This is not a job that someone does when they "get around to it," or when they have nothing better to do.

3. **Follow-up.** Following up on direct mail to businesses by phone will raise your success rate in getting appointments by at least fivefold. This follow-up is most effectively done by your marketing person, as opposed to a technician or professional.

If you're marketing business-to-business, do your telephone follow-up during the working day. Don't use a script, just be friendly and try to get an appointment. If you're courteous and low-key, people will usually respond in kind.

> "Nothing great was ever achieved without enthusiasm."
> —Ralph Waldo Emerson

Your Mail Package

You should now select a format for your direct mail. The mail piece will normally be a letter in a standard envelope. For certain types of messages, especially to large numbers of recipients, a post card may be equally effective and certainly less costly. Here are some suggestions about format:

The letter. Print the letter on your regular stationery and make it look as good as normal correspondence that you would send to a client. If you use substandard paper or substandard printing, it will reflect negatively on your firm and your image.

Envelope. Make sure that the envelope is a business envelope with your normal logo on it. Using your laser printer, print each address directly onto the envelope. This will make it look like a normal business letter, and people generally open business-looking letters. We recommend that you use first-class mail. Letters going out with a label or bulk mail postage will result in a lower response rate.

Response card. People receiving direct mail are often hesitant about calling the sender on the phone because they don't wish to commit themselves. On the other hand, they may be interested in whatever you are offering. Therefore, include a postage-paid business reply card that people can fill out and send in without incurring any risk or obligation.

Other materials. To increase the effectiveness of your mailing, you might include promotional items such as:

- a small brochure
- a copy of your yellow page ad
- a copy of a newspaper advertisement
- a copy of an article that features you or your company
- a small item that makes the envelope lumpy
- anything that catches the recipient's eye and gets attention

Obtaining Names and Addresses

A key task is finding the names and addresses of potential clients. You can compile mailing lists yourself from a variety of sources, including:

- newspapers
- magazines
- yellow pages
- real estate agents
- trade directories
- title companies
- insurance agents
- utility companies, and
- the local recording office, such as city hall

Or you can purchase lists from mailing list brokers or the phone company.

As all direct mail books point out, it's important to test different lists, letters, and offers. Keep accurate and detailed records of your direct mail program so that you can track your response rates over time. You'll then be able to see which offers work best for which audiences.

PUBLIC RELATIONS

Public relations are another important part of your marketing effort. Here are four different activities to incorporate in your "marketing machine":

Congratulatory Letters. Make everyone in your office responsible for being a "clipping service." Ask them to clip out anything they see in the newspaper related to a client or friend of the firm and to give it to the marketing coordinator. He or she is then responsible for drafting an appropriate letter of congratulations.

Announcing Changes. Whether it's adding new people, adding new services, or changing locations, let people know about it. View these changes as a marketing opportunity—yet another chance to remind clients and friends of who you are and what you do.

Press Releases. They are inexpensive, take little time to prepare, and can be effective when done consistently. It is important to set up a system for generating press releases so that you don't "reinvent the wheel" each time something noteworthy happens. Plan on sending out a press release at least every calendar quarter.

Tips for Preparing a Good Press Release

- Keep it short—one page is usually sufficient.
- Double space it.
- Enclose a 3" × 5" black and white photograph, whenever possible. Label the photo on the back stating what the picture is about and give name, address and phone number.
- Address the press release to the name and title of the appropriate person.
- Write "For Immediate Release" up at the top left.
- The headline should be underlined and briefly summarize the information in the text.
- Be factual in your wording. Avoid unnecessary elaboration.
- Answer WHO-WHAT-WHEN-WHERE-HOW and WHY in the first paragraph.
- Flesh out the details in the following paragraph(s).
- Send a brochure, background on the firm or background on the subject matter as appropriate, in order to validate yourself, the firm and the event.
- End the press release with "# # #" to indicate there are no more pages to follow.

Public Speaking Requests. Public speaking is a great opportunity to attract new clients and it's very efficient—you can pitch a large number of prospects at the same time.

There are lots of groups that use outside speakers, including:
- chambers of commerce
- adult education classes
- service clubs (Rotary, Lions, Roundtable, etc.)
- trade groups
- social clubs

But don't wait for them to call you! There's competition for these speaking slots. Send letters to these organizations and follow up by phone.

NEWSLETTERS

Many companies report success from publishing a newsletter. This isn't the first thing I would recommend you do since it takes considerable time and effort, but it is an excellent way of keeping your name in front of all customers, all prospects, and all referral sources. Send a newsletter out three or four times per year and make it as colorful and jazzy as you can.

As to content, make it readable and interesting. Here are some suggestions:

- A letter from you letting the reader know your business is doing well and that you are looking for more clients.

- A spotlight on one of your employees or co-workers. People love human interest stories and it's an opportunity to showcase your talents.

- An article about one of your customers. Customers are usually thrilled to be featured, will do most of the writing for you, and will ask for extra copies to send to their own customers and prospects. (If they don't ask, suggest it!)

- A paragraph describing the most recent speech you (or a colleague) made, and emphasizing that you are always available to make presentations to groups.

- Special interest items that might include cartoons, photographs, puzzles, or recipes. A favorite newsletter from a CPA firm includes movie reviews— clearly not related to their services, but of immediate and universal appeal and now a regular feature.

- A little technical stuff is OK too, although, as you have observed, the principal thrust should be human interest.

IMPLEMENTING YOUR MARKETING PROGRAM

All of this sounds like a lot of work, doesn't it? It is, but most of it is relatively routine and can be easily systematized as discussed in the previous chapter. When you have a system in place, it's easier to get things done. To help you implement your marketing program, you should also do these two things:

- Hire a marketing coordinator; and
- Install a contact management database system.

Hire a Marketing Coordinator

Regardless of the size of your company, my advice is to hire someone to coordinate your various marketing activities.

This person can be either full-time or part-time and should focus initially on organizing the direct mail program—making sure that all marketing correspondence gets out on time and that the required follow-up, including telemarketing, is done on a timely basis.

Install a Contact Management System

Your marketing activities will generate a significant number of contacts and you will need a way of dealing with them effectively.

"Motivation is what gets you started. Habit is what keeps you going."
—Jim Ryan, runner

A contact management database program is the answer. There are a number of popular programs, such as ACT!, Goldmine, and Maximizer. These are readily available at computer stores.

In addition to maintaining names and addresses, these programs have numerous capabilities which are important for marketing:

- Ability to tag each name with multiple attributes such as client/nonclient, industry, profession, specialty, year-end, birthday, SIC code, and responsible individual;

- Ability to sort and create lists by one or more attributes. For example, your program could quickly identify all litigation specialist lawyers in a given city;

- A reminder system that tells you when to follow-up on a mail piece—this feature is essential for telemarketing;

- A note-taking function where you can summarize all conversations with a contact. You can also "attach" documents to a name.

The modest investment required for contact management software will pay for itself many times over in marketing results.

ACTION SUMMARY

"Not only strike while the iron is hot, but make it hot by striking."
—Oliver Cromwell

1 Decide what customers you want to serve and what products or services you want to offer them.

2 Set up a 3-day-a-week lunch or breakfast program. Take out your clients, friends, and other "centers of influence."

3 Update your brochure, product information sheets, and firm's image.

4 Get a Web site.

5 Put together a kit with useful information that you can use as a "freebie" or premium.

6 Do targeted direct mail every week.

7 Follow up your direct mail with phone calls.

8 Send out press releases.

9 Develop an effective newsletter.

10 Hire a marketing coordinator.

11 Install a contact management database system.

12 Write a simple marketing action plan and just do it!

YOUR TOTAL ACTION PLAN

Now that you are familiar with the main components of an effective marketing program, you are ready for action.

In this brief book, there are many ideas. If you

are in business for yourself, you owe it to yourself to set up a systematic marketing plan. By making marketing routine, it will become easier and easier to do.

If you are an employee of a business, we hope you've seen many reasons why marketing can benefit you in your job. Building better relationships with customers and prospects will make your job more fun well as increase your value to the company.

Following are seven steps to begin implementing your overall marketing efforts.

1 Review all of the ideas in this chapter and in the rest of the book.

2 Select 6-10 ideas that suit your business, your customers, and your style of doing business.

3 Write up a marketing action plan. (We call it that because it's big on action, not theory.) For each marketing initiative, document:
- Who's going to do it?
- When is it to be done?
- What's the approved budget?
- What other resources are needed?
- Where does it take place (if it's an event)?

4 Monitor progress on a regular basis.

5 Get everyone involved and reward people for marketing.

6 Celebrate your accomplishments with all of your team members.

7 Repeat the successful things and experiment with new ideas.

Follow these steps and you will create a first-class marketing machine! Don't delay—more marketing programs flounder because of indecision than for any other cause and failure to implement.

In the words of Dr. Tom Peters, *"Ready! Fire! Aim!"*

REFERENCES AND RECOMMENDED READINGS

Albrecht, K. (1992). *The Only Thing That Matters: Bringing the Power of the Customer into the Center of Your Business.* New York: Harper Business.

Barlow, J., & Møller, C. (1996). *A Complaint Is a Gift.* San Francisco: Berrett-Koehler Publishers, Inc.

Berry, L.L. (1995). *On Great Service: A Framework for Action.* New York: Free Press.

Blades, B.. (1998). Using Creativity in the Sales Process: Step Out of Your Rut and Up to Success. In R. Crandall (Ed.), *Break-Out Creativity: Bringing Creativity to the Workplace.* Corte Madera, CA: Association for Innovation in Management.

Blanchard, K., & Johnson, S. (1981). *The One Minute Manager.* New York: William Morrow & Company.

Blanchard, K., & Bowles, S. (1993). *Raving Fans* New York: William Morrow & Company.

Brody, M., & Pachter, B. (1994). *Business Etiquette.* Homewood, IL: Irwin Professional Publishing.

Byham, W.C. (1990). *Zapp! The Lightning of Empowerment.* New York: Harmony Books.

Carlzon, Jan. (1987). *Moments of Truth.* Cambridge, MA: Ballinger Publishing Co., 1987.

Considine, R., and Cohn, T. (1996). *WAYMISH: Why Are You Making It So Hard for Me to Give You My Money?* Pasadena, CA: WAYMISH Publishing Co.

Crandall, R. (1996). *Marketing Your Services: For People Who Hate to Sell.* Chicago: Contemporary Books.

Crandall, R. (1998). *1001 Ways to Market Your Services: For People Who Hate to Sell.* Chicago: Contemporary/NTC.

Cross, R., & Smith, J. (1996). *Customer Bonding: Pathway to Lasting Customer Loyalty.* NTC Publishing Group.

Fracassi, L.F. (1997). Three Ways to Serve Your Customers and Sell More. In. R. Crandall (Ed.).*10 Secrets of Marketing Success: How to Jump-Start Your Marketing* (pp. 63-80). Corte Madera, CA: Select Press.

Gerber, M.E. (1994). *The E-Myth Revisited: Why Most Small Business Still Don't Work & What You Can Do about Yours.* New York: HarperBusiness.

Hanan, M. (1989). *Key Account Selling* (2nd ed.). New York: AMACOM.

Hanan, M. (1995). *Consultative Selling (5th Ed.).* New York: AMACOM.

Kawasaki, G. (1993). *Selling the Dream: How to Use Everyday Evangelism to Promote Your Product, Company, or Ideas & Make a Difference.* New York: HarperCollins.

Kinnear, T.C., & Bernhardt, K.L. (1983). *Principles of Marketing.* Glenview, IL: Scott Foresman.

Kroc, R. (1990). *Grinding It Out: The Making of McDonald's.* New York: St. Martin.

Levinson, J.C. (1985). *Guerrilla Marketing.* Boston: Houghton-Mifflin.

Levinson, J.C. (1990). *Guerrilla Marketing Weapons: 100 Affordable Marketing Methods for Maximizing Profits from Your Small Business.* New York: Plume Books.

Levitt, T. (1981). *Marketing for Business Growth.* New York: McGraw-Hill.

Mackay, H. (1989) *Swim with the Sharks Without Being Eaten Alive.* New York: William Morrow & Company.

Mackay, H. (1997). *Dig Your Well Before You're Thirsty: The Only Networking Book You'll Ever Need.* New York: Currency/Doubleday.

Mandino, O. (1989). *The Greatest Salesman in the World.* New York: Bantam.

McCormack, M.H. (1985). *What They Don't Teach You at Harvard Business School.* New York: Bantam.

Nelson, Bob. (1995). *1001 Ways to Reward Employees.* New York: Workman.

Ogilvy, D. (1985). *Ogilvy on Advertising.* New York: Vintage.

Peppers, D., & Rogers, M. (1993). *The One to One Future: Building Relationships One Customer at a Time.* New York: Doubleday.

Phillips, M., & Raspberry, S. (1986). *Marketing Without Advertising.* Berkeley, CA: Nolo Press.

Peters, T. (1995). *The Tom Peters Seminar: Crazy Times Call for Crazy Organizations.* New York: Vintage.

Rackham, N. (1988). *Spin Selling.* New York: McGraw-Hill.

Reichheld, F.F. (with T. Teal). (1996). *The Loyalty Effect.* Boston: Harvard Business School Press.

Rhode, J. (1997). Secrets of Successful Referral Source Management. In. R. Crandall (Ed.). *10 Secrets of Marketing Success: How to Jump-Start Your Marketing* (pp. 225-246). Corte Madera, CA: Select Press.

Ries, A. (1997). *Focus: The Future of Your Company Depends on It.* New York: HarperBusiness.

Ries, A., & Trout, J. (1981). *Positioning: The Battle for Your Mind.* New York: McGraw-Hill.

Rosenbluth, H.F., & Peters, D. McFerrin. (1992). *The Customer Comes Second.* New York: William Morrow.

Salam, W. (1997). In R. Crandall (Ed.). The Power of Personal Notes: 35 Ways to Say 'Thank You' and Stay in Touch. *Marketing Magic: Proven Pathways to Success* (pp. 341-370). Corte Madera, CA: Select Press.

Stanley, T.J. (1993). *Networking with the Affluent and their Advisors.* Homewood, IL: Business One Irwin.

Stone, M., Davies, D., & Bond, A. (1996). *Direct Hits: Direct Marketing with a Winning Edge.* Landham, MD: Pitman Publications.

Trout, J. (with S. Rivkin). (1995). *The New Positioning.* New York: McGraw-Hill.

Whitely, R., & Hessan, D. (1996). *Customer-Centered Growth.* Reading, MA: Addison-Wesley.

Wilson, J.R. (1994). *Word of Mouth Marketing.* New York: Wiley.

INDEX